Britain's Railways in Colour

BR Steam in the 1950s and 1960s

Haynes Publishing

Britain's Railways in Colour

BR Steam in the 1950s and 1960s

Colin G. Maggs MBE

First published in August 2009

A catalogue record for this book is available from the British Library

ISBN 978 1 84425 650 1

Library of Congress catalog card no. 2009923202

Design and layout by Dominic Stickland

Haynes North America Inc., 861 Lawrence Drive, Newbury Park, California 91320, USA

Published by Haynes Publishing, Sparkford, Yeovil, Somerset BA22 7JJ, UK.
Tel: 01963 442030 Fax: 01963 440001
Int. tel: +44 1963 442030
Int. fax: +44 1963 440001
E-mail: sales@haynes.co.uk
Website: www.haynes.co.uk

Printed and bound in the UK

ACKNOWLEDGEMENTS

Special thanks are due to Colin Roberts for checking the text and amplifying the captions.

Colin G. Maggs MBE, 2009

Contents

Introduction

The photographs in this book come from my own collection and those of my friends whose transparencies are now in my care. We all lived in the Bath area, so the pictures are therefore weighted towards the southern half of England, although we made some forays into splendid northern climes. The titles of the areas into which the images have been grouped are necessarily broad and so only samples can be offered of each area.

In the 1950s and '60s the attitude of railway photographers towards colour was totally different from today. In 2009, a cameraman taking a colour picture will know that if it appears in a book, journal or newspaper, it is likely to be reproduced in colour. Not so in those days when colour printing was expensive, so almost all the reproductions were in black and white. Black and white film was cheaper – a serious consideration when every penny counted. It also had a faster speed than contemporary colour film – original Kodachrome was rated at 10 ASA. If your lens was limited to f4.5 and your pocket would not allow anything better, you were limited to an exposure of one hundredth of a second, which was only suitable for shots of stationary, or slow-moving trains.

These facts meant that black and white was the principal format but some enthusiasts used a second camera loaded with colour film, just for their own private, or railway society viewing in mind, rather than publication. The arrival of Kodachrome II, in about 1962, with a speed of 25 ASA, was helpful and gave a little more scope for photographing moving trains.

Another factor affecting photography in the Fifties and Sixties was transport. Private cars were very much a luxury which could not be afforded by everyone. This meant that some were restricted to walking, cycling, or using a train or bus which of course took more time than using a car and therefore restricted possible photographic locations. A further factor was that many in employment worked a 5½-day week, so only a Saturday afternoon and evening were available for railway photography as Sunday train services were generally sparse.

In the era depicted in this book, particularly from about 1963 onwards, locomotives, unless recently ex-works or specially cleaned for a rail tour, tended to be grimy through lack of staff to keep the paintwork spotless. They were certainly unlike the immaculate engines seen on today's preserved railways, which to a certain extent, give a false impression of how things were.

In addition to depicting the locomotives themselves, these pictures show much of the now changed infrastructure: mechanical signals and signalboxes, gas and oil lamps, barrow crossings, water columns, and tanks. Even something as simple as a locomotive running round its train is rarely seen today on the national network.

This was an interesting period, especially the Fifties, as Grouping, and even pre-Grouping locomotives and rolling stock were to be seen, although with the spread of dieselisation or electrification, these were rapidly being withdrawn and BR Standards supplanted them. Coaching stock livery could vary, and apart from non-corridor red stock, there were corridors in 'blood and custard' (carmine and cream), green appeared on many SR steam-hauled passenger coaches, and the WR's principal express trains were in GWR chocolate and cream. Branch lines were in abundance and one came across them every few miles, offering such delights as push-pull trains and pick-up goods.

Today's freight trains are generally specialised, carrying just one commodity such as a nuclear flask, or bulk traffic like stone, coal, or oil. In the Fifties and Sixties, railways were still general carriers and a considerable proportion of goods sold in local shops came by rail: biscuits, books, cakes, chocolate, clothing, dairy produce, greengrocery, grocery, ironmongery, meat, newspapers and magazines, sweets and tobacco.

A large factory often had its own private siding, or sidings. To prevent industry from using wagons and vans for free storage space, customers were allowed 48 hours for a wagon to be emptied, or 72 if carrying coal or coke. If a wagon exceeded this time allowance, a daily demurrage charge was incurred, which was very fair as a wagon still under load deprived the railway of its use and therefore loss of revenue.

Some private sidings, or even BR yards in congested sites, had sidings accessed by small turntables. There were several methods for moving wagons without a locomotive: a horse, shunting tractor, pinch bar, hydraulic or electrically operated powered capstan, or a truck mover propelled by an air-cooled engine which also operated a powerful hydraulic ram that locked the truck mover securely between the rail and the wagon's underframe. Today shunting is a thing of the past.

Country stations often had delightful gardens and some

country stationmasters saw that fresh flowers were on the waiting room table and books and magazines were available for waiting passengers. On the other hand, city stations in the steam age tended to be dull and dismal, partly due to the constant pall of smoke, to a large extent caused by the railway itself, while the architectural delights of the buildings could not be enjoyed because they were buried beneath layers of grime. Today, multi-coloured bricks really are multi-coloured; platform canopy supports may have features picked out in various hues; flowers may be in hanging baskets or in tubs set between the tracks or on the platforms.

Goods stations with hand cranes have disappeared as has the parcels department of passenger stations. There were railway-owned vans and lorries, quite often of the mechanical horse and trailer variety, to deliver and collect goods travelling by rail. Farmers' tractors appeared in goods yards to collect sugar beet pulp or fertilisers. Most stations had a cattle pen and an end-loading dock for wheeled vehicles. Boxes of fish decanted from trains were left on the platform for collection by local merchants. Tickets, sold at booking offices rather than travel centres, were colour-coded and exciting to collect, unlike the bland offering of today.

In this period that vital, although very often literally overlooked part of the railway, the permanent way, was undergoing change. Bullhead rail, fixed in chairs by means of keys, was being replaced by flat-bottomed rail, meaning that the ganger patrolling his length with a hammer to knock in loose keys, became redundant. Yellow track machines grew an ever-more regular sight.

Today, the country station has all but disappeared. Until the 1960s the local stationmaster was a man of importance, a little below the squire in rank, but roughly on a par with the local parson and headmaster. He cultivated the friendship of nearby farmers and industrialists to win freight traffic for his station, and with the vicar and headmaster to gain potential excursion traffic. Even a country stationmaster was in charge of a small empire: probably at least one booking clerk, two porters (one on early and the other on late turn); perhaps a lad porter, and two or three signalmen. Staff were often imaginative, using blackboard and chalk, designing attractive notices advertising excursions, or distributing local pocket timetables. Employment on the railway generally received better pay than working on the land, offered the opportunity of advancement, and until the Beeching era, was a job for life if you kept to the rules.

Signalboxes were a great feature of the railway. Generally set every few miles, the signal arms gave the railway observer a clue as to when a train might be expected. Signalmen took a pride in keeping their box sparkling clean: levers, floor, brasswork and windows all kept spotless. Woe betide a railwayman who came in with muddy boots! A signalbox was a magical place with its instruments and bells and I remember bribing my way into the local box with some windfall stewing pears. A signalbox could be a very pleasant place to work with breath-taking views. On the other hand, with so much glass, temperatures could be extreme: very hot in summer and very cold in winter. Although a box was always supplied with coal for heating, this was not always sufficient and it was not unknown for a signalman, in exchange for a cup of tea, to beg some coal from a driver when an engine halted at a signal.

Good arguments can be made for and against the rapid scrapping of British steam locomotives, many of which were modern and could have been used for a further 20 or 30 years. Enthusiasts were sad to see them go, for they marked the end of a glorious era. Today, we must be grateful for those enthusiasts who have taken enormous time, trouble and not inconsiderable expense, to preserve so many locomotives and bring them back into working order for all to enjoy.

This collection of pictures is intended to be savoured again and again. Just as with a painting, you are invited to come back and see fresh things and are not intended to take it all in at one quick glance!

Colin G. Maggs MBE
August 2009

South Devon

South Devon was particularly favoured by railway photographers in steam days. Why? It was in a delightful, often sunny holiday area, so the wife and children could be parked happily on the beach while the cameraman went off to take pictures. And what a wide choice was available including 14 miles of main line beside water, from Powderham, just below Exeter, to Newton Abbot, with the possibility of waves breaking over the track. If one sought a change, there were delightful branch lines to savour: Heathfield to Exeter; Newton Abbot to Moretonhampstead; Churston to Brixham; Totnes to Ashburton; Brent to Kingsbridge and Plymouth to Princetown. The photogenic Churston to Kingswear line ran beside the River Dart and offered many opportunities.

Inland the main line was far from dull. Engines could be seen and most definitely heard, tackling the 1-in-35 Dainton bank, while west of Totnes they faced the 1-in-45 Rattery bank. These locations had the advantage that speeds here were low, so if your lens was small, the shutter speed slow, or the weather dull, slow movement offered the chance of a crisp picture. Unless a train was short, these severe gradients demanded passenger trains to be double-headed so you got two engines for the price of one. Goods trains were banked at the rear, giving the photographer a chance to wind on his film after he had taken the front engine and be ready to photograph the one at the back.

Summer Saturdays were fantastic – a continuous procession of trains along the main lines, either literally block-to-block or almost so; an enthusiast not having to wait long for the next train. If there was a dearth of passenger or mixed traffic locomotives, on some Saturdays, a '28XX' class 2-8-0 freight engine would be pressed into passenger service. Such a choice would be unpopular with following trains as they were not so speedy as a mixed traffic or express passenger engine, and would delay progress of the trains behind.

Branch lines offered the delights of auto-train working. Those trains obviated the need for the locomotive to run round at termini, thus saving effort and time of both engine crew and signalman. The fact that the engine pushed the coach in one direction and thus remained at the rear of the train, looked a little peculiar and so was attractive. Not all photographers liked them though because the engine was leading only half the time. Some of the auto trailers were particularly interesting as they had been converted from steam rail motors. Steam rail motors had fallen out of use as they were inflexible and unable to cope with extra traffic, so were replaced by a small tank engine and auto coach, or coaches, a separate locomotive and a varying number of coaches being much more capable of coping with an influx of passengers.

The livery of the GWR was well chosen – the green locomotives with polished brass and copper, together with chocolate and cream-coloured coaches complemented the West Country scenery and somehow LMS maroon, or LNER teak would have been out of place.

Unfortunately, the Beeching axe of 1963 closed most of these branch lines, but it is fortunate that we can still savour a GWR example between Buckfastleigh and Littlehempston where it is like turning the clock back 60 or more years, the only difference being that trains are better patronised now than they were then.

Most railway photographers classified trains in order of what they considered were important: express passenger, stopping passenger, freight, and industrial. Although there were three interesting industrial branches in South Devon, my friends and myself ignored them unfortunately, perhaps because we were unaware of their existence.

One such line was the Exeter City Basin branch which lasted until 1983. Broad gauge traffic began in 1887, with standard gauge wagons not using the mixed-gauge line until 1876. A City Basin train then consisted of broad and standard gauge wagons linked by a match truck with extra wide buffers suitable to meet the buffers of both gauges without interlocking. The coupling chain slid on a transverse bar. Even as late as 1962 the line handled 54,762 tons of freight, 53,066 tons being 'motor spirit'.

The Teignmouth Quay branch dealt principally with inwards coal, timber and wood pulp, with clay outwards. Railway locomotives were prohibited from using the quay. At first horses were used, then a rather unsuccessful petrol tractor and finally a Sentinel steam road tractor fitted with timber baulks to act as buffers. Named *The Elephant* it was fortunately preserved.

The three quarters of a mile-long Totnes Quay branch, in addition to serving the quay where timber was imported, also served the cattle market and several industrial premises.

⬆️ A stopping train hauled by 'Hall' class 4-6-0 No. 5981 *Frensham Hall* ascends the 1 in 71 between Goodrington Sands Halt and Churston on the Kingswear line. The concrete pillars to the right of the track are line monuments buried securely in the ballast so that they will not shift. Cast into the top was an old fishplate with a cut in it. Measurement was taken between the cut and the top of the rail to facilitate the track's alignment to its original position. 'Halls' were useful mixed traffic engines and were often seen on freight trains during the week and on the many extra passenger trains run on summer Saturdays. The fact that they were being hauled by a mixed traffic engine was concealed from the passengers by them being named. The fireman is smiling at the photographer. *(R. E. Toop)*

↖ Another 'Hall' class 4-6-0, No. 5992 *Horton Hall*, approaches Kingswear tender first with a stopping train. The boundary fence is unusually close to the permanent way due to the river being nearby on the right with space at a premium. *(R. E. Toop)*

← No. 5992 runs round the train at Kingswear, passing a fine example of a bracket signal to the left. *(R. E. Toop)*

→ The paintwork is in splendid condition and the brasswork is shining in the sun as No. 5992 receives attention at Kingswear. The driver is taking the opportunity to apply oil before the return journey. There is a spare lamp on its bracket by the smokebox. Beyond the engine are BR Standard non-corridor coaches, with corridor coaches in the far carriage sidings. Many coaches of the period were only used on summer Saturday trains, taking holidaymakers to and from resorts. *(R. E. Toop)*

An ex-GWR 1400 class 0-4-2T, No. 1427, propels a modern auto coach en route from Brixham to Churston. on 10 August 1955. Push-and-pull operation avoided having to uncouple the locomotive and running round – tiresome for both engine crew and signalman. It also saved time if a branch train was running late due to a delay waiting for a connecting main line train. When the engine pushed the coach, the fireman remained on the footplate and in addition to his usual tasks of firing and controlling the boiler water level, he was additionally responsible for altering the cut-off and operating the large ejector to release the brakes. The driver took a stance in the control compartment of the coach. The coach carries a gong on the end to give warning as a whistle on the engine could not always be heard when pushing. Here, the driver can be seen waving to the photographer. *(R. E. Toop)*

Churchward 4500 class 2-6-2T No. 4555 stands at Buckfastleigh on 29 August 1967, on the preserved Dart Valley Railway, today's South Devon Railway. The first passenger train for 11 years ran from Buckfastleigh to Totnes on 5 April 1969 and the line was officially reopened by Dr Richard Beeching, the man responsible for closing so many branch lines, on 21 May that year. The express headcode is inappropriate. To the left is a corrugated iron pagoda, favoured by the GWR, and the engine in the distance is 1400 class 0-4-2T No. 1420. *(R. E. Toop)*

Collett 4575 class 2-6-2T No. 5525 breasting the summit of the incline with a Kingsbridge to Brent train. The 4575s differed from the earlier 4500s in having sloping tops to the side tanks giving them an increased water capacity. Firemen on GWR stopping trains sometimes placed the lamp above the coupling hook rather than by the chimney which was a labour-saving device when an engine had to run round its train frequently. The board reading 'All Down Goods and Mineral Trains Must Stop Dead Here' was required as the brakes had to be pinned down at the head of the gradient to keep the train under control. On the left is a permanent way hut, its windows supposedly secured against vandals. The door was normally locked to prevent theft of tools, but on one branch known to the author, the huts were left unlocked over the weekend because if secured, local miners always broke the lock so as to enter to play cards on Sundays, using an upturned bucket as a table. *(R. E. Toop)*

'Large Prairie', 5101 class 2-6-2T No. 5148 arrives at Kingswear with a train from Newton Abbot including some coaches as repainted in 1957 by BR (Western Region) in chocolate and cream for principal expresses. Built as 3100 class No. 3148 in March 1906, this locomotive was altered to the 5101 class in April 1928, the difference being in detail. It was not withdrawn until December 1959 and when seen on the 'Dump' at Swindon it was still remarkably clean. The picturesque line between Paignton and Kingswear is run today as the Paignton & Dartmouth Steam Railway, Kingswear being the station for Dartmouth, which is reached by ferry. *(R. E. Toop)*

↗ Quite of few of the 5101 class 2-6-2Ts were used on banking duties and here No. 5164 assists a down freight from Totnes up the 1 in 65 of Rattery bank. The rear wagons are well buffered up. 'RU' on the brake van stands for 'Restricted User', meaning that it was required to be returned to its home station. Some guards preferred a BR Standard brake van with a veranda at each end and ducket where they could look out from the comfort of the interior and the hand brake was placed inside, not on the veranda as on the GWR 'Toad'. The concrete posts of the fencing, would have been cast at the GWR's concrete works at Taunton. The box van adjoining the brake van has a leaking roof, so its contents are protected by a sheet. No. 5164 is now preserved on the Severn Valley Railway. *(R. E. Toop)*

↑ A Paddington to Plymouth train ascends Rattery bank with 'Castle' class 4-6-0 No. 5034 *Corfe Castle* piloted by No. D6314, a 1,000hp Type 2 North British diesel-hydraulic carrying two white discs for the headcode. The coaching stock is of varying colours – the new BR maroon livery, the old 'blood and custard' (carmine and cream) and the brown and cream carried by principal WR expresses. The drainage ditch parallel with the fence is neatly kept and the track recently re-ballasted. On the left of the diesel is a permanent way hut. *(R. E. Toop)*

A 'Castle' piloted by a 'Hall' descend the bank beyond Rattery signalbox with an up express. The train engine's safety valves are blowing off. (*R. E. Toop*)

'Hall' class 4-6-0 No. 5967 *Bickmarsh Hall* pilots an unrecorded 'King', approaching Dainton summit with a down train. The bank, in places as steep as 1 in 36, was taxing and curves increased the resistance. The permanent way men take a rest while waiting for the train to pass. No. 5967 is preserved, with restoration only recently commenced, at the Northampton & Lamport Railway. (*R. E. Toop*)

'Grange' class 4-6-0 No. 6831 *Bearley Grange* passes Tigley signalbox on Rattery bank. The gradient has eased here to 1 in 90. The 'Granges' were introduced in 1936 and were similar to the 'Halls', but with 5ft 8in diameter wheels instead of 6ft. They used the wheels and motion of withdrawn 4300 class 2-6-0s. (*R. E. Toop*)

With a stopping train to Kingswear, 4-6-0 No. 5994 *Roydon Hall* climbs towards Churston, the line from Goodrington Sands being as steep as 1 in 60 at one point. Despite this, steam is issuing from the safety valve. (*R. E. Toop*)

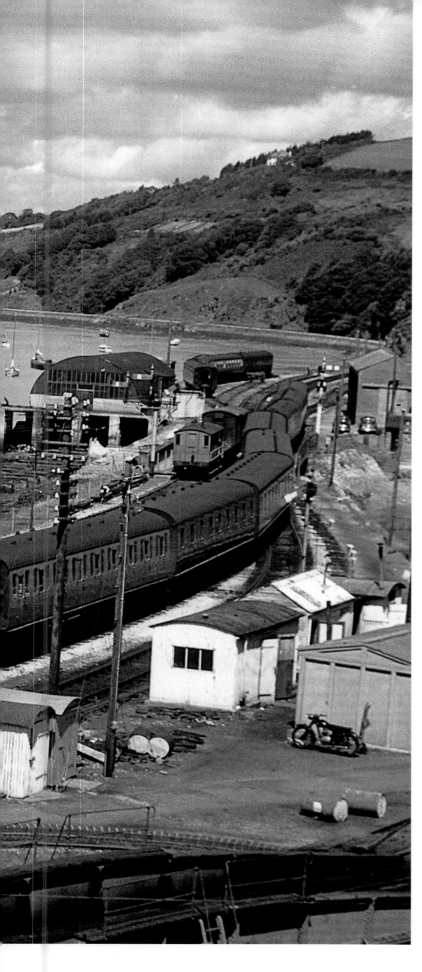

Class 6100 2-6-2T No. 6146 arrives at Kingswear with a stopping train. This class was similar to the 5101s except the boiler pressure was increased from 200lb to 225lb psi, thus increasing its tractive effort. The boiler plates were of the same dimensions, but of a higher-tensile nickel steel. The leading coach is an ex-LMS corridor brake second, but the second and third coaches are of compartment type. The signalman in the large, timber-built box enjoys a splendid view across to Dartmouth. In the right-hand corner can be seen several typical GWR corrugated iron huts by the turntable. *(R. E. Toop)*

The Remainder of
Devon & West Somerset

East Devon was served by the Southern Railway, while the GWR served most of North Devon, although the SR covered North West Devon. Exeter St David's was one of the change-over places with the curiosity of a GWR up express to London facing the same direction as an SR down train from London.

As the SR main line to Exeter kept well inland, branches served the resorts of Lyme Regis (actually in Dorset), Seaton, Sidmouth, Budleigh Salterton and Exmouth. On weekdays each of the branches would be served by a through coach, or coaches to or from Waterloo, while on summer Saturdays a whole train might be provided. Exeter to Exmouth is still very much a thriving branch with commuter traffic and offers a delightful run beside the River Exe. The Seaton to Colyton branch has been re-laid with 2ft 9in gauge track and worked as an electric tramway, principally as a tourist attraction but to a certain extent used as a local transport facility. Exmouth, Budleigh Salterton and Seaton stations were situated conveniently close to the beach, but due to gradients, Lyme Regis station was located at the top of a hill as was Sidmouth, the latter was deliberately placed some distance from the sea in order to deter rowdy trippers.

From Exeter St David's the SR ran northwards and then its main line bore west and south to Okehampton and beside the River Tamar down to Plymouth. Perhaps short-sightedly, the line between Meldon Quarry and Bere Alston closed on 6 May 1968. A shuttle service then operated between Exeter and Okehampton, but this was withdrawn from 5 June 1972, since when it has been reopened as a tourist line. At the time of writing, a group is advocating the reopening of the line from Bere Alston to Tavistock.

From Yeoford Junction, the SR continued north to Barnstaple where branches ran to Bideford and Ilfracombe and a delightful 1ft 11½in gauge line served Lynton. Although the latter closed in 1935 preservationists have recently reopened a length near Woody Bay and propose opening further sections. The Ilfracombe branch was noted for its sharp curves and steep gradients – 2 miles of 1 in 36 starting from Ilfracombe station perched on a ledge above the town.

Although most of North Devon was Southern territory, the GWR ran from Norton Fitzwarren, west of Taunton, along the southern edge of Exmoor to Barnstaple, from there exercising running powers to Ilfracombe. Although most people would have considered it a branch line, the GWR marked it on their official map as a main line. Before myxomatosis halted the traffic, many rabbits were despatched by rail, their scent lingering after a train had passed.

From Morebath Junction a branch followed the River Exe to Tiverton Junction. 'Junction', like 'road' used as a suffix, indicated to the initiated that the station was some distance from the place it was named after, the uninitiated believing it to be just a stone's throw away. From Tiverton Junction another branch ran up the Culm Valley to Hemyock. The Culm Valley Light Railway was one of the first to be constructed under the Regulation of Railways Act 1868 which allowed light railways, defined as a line with a maximum weight of 8 tons per axle and a speed of 25mph. Permanent way was lighter than that used on a main line and stations could be simply a platform and shed. This meant that a light railway could be constructed relatively cheaply in an area where an ordinary line would be uneconomic. The population of the communities served was 6,610 and the line was estimated to cost £3,000 a mile, comparing very favourably with the Cheddar Valley line at £12,000 a mile. In the event, the CVLR cost about £6,000 per mile. Income was insufficient to pay interest on the overdraft and certainly nothing was available for ordinary shareholders who had been promised about 5 per cent. The only solution was to sell to the GWR. The branch, which received scant attention from enthusiasts, was sharply curved and needed to be worked by light, short-wheelbase engines (latterly the '14XX' 0-4-2Ts) and short bogie coaches. The maximum speed of 15mph was too low to charge the coach lighting batteries and so they were gas lit. Passenger services were withdrawn from 9 September 1963 but considerable milk traffic continued until 31 October 1975.

Durston, on the Bristol to Taunton line, was interesting. Originally it was the junction of the branch to Yeovil, but when the new shorter route from Reading to Taunton was created early in the 20th century using existing and new lines, the junction for Yeovil left the new line at Curry Rivel Junction. Nevertheless trains between Taunton and Yeovil continued to be routed via Durston rather than taking the direct route.

The former broad gauge Cheddar Valley branch left the Bristol & Exeter mainline at Yatton and proceeded to Wells where the East Somerset Railway formed an extension to join the Bathampton and Chippenham line to Weymouth line at Witham. The CVR, owned by the B&ER was a financial success. Apart from items sent to shops, coal and builders' merchants, passenger traffic was boosted by tourists visiting Cheddar Gorge. Cheddar station was considered so important that it was given an overall roof, a rarity for a through branch line station. Milk traffic was heavy, each passenger train having at least one van, the Sunday train conveying eight vans.

The introduction of the Royal Sovereign variety of strawberry about 1900 which travelled well, meant that strawberries grown in the area could be sent to distant markets in South Wales, the Midlands, the North and even Scotland. Vans containing strawberries left a pleasant scent as they passed. Another important source of traffic on the Yatton to Witham line was stone, and indeed, part of the East Somerset section of the line remains open for this traffic.

Another West Country light railway was the Wrington Vale branch built by the GWR and opened as late as 4 December 1901. This area was used for dairy farming and the railway enabled milk, butter and cheese to be swiftly carried to urban markets in the days before rapid road transport. The line branched from the Cheddar Valley line to Congresbury. Most of its level crossings were ungated, but the track was protected by cattle grids. Trains were subject to a maximum speed of 25mph with a lower limit of 10mph at ungated level crossings. For economy the railway followed the lie of the land and few cuttings and embankments were made. It cost about £3,000 a mile. Except on a gradient of 1 in 50 where bullhead rail was used to prevent rail creep, rails were flat-bottomed and spiked directly to the sleepers. A bus service begun in 1921 caused passengers to desert the railway as it was both quicker and cheaper to travel the 11 miles from Blagdon to Bristol by road rather than the 19¾ miles by rail, which also involved the inconvenience of changing trains at Yatton. Passenger traffic was withdrawn on 14 September 1931, and it was one of the first lines in the area to lose such a service. The line closed to goods beyond Wrington on 1 November 1950, and to Wrington on 10 June 1963.

Ivatt LMS-design Class 2 2-6-2T No. 41292 at Lyme Regis, Dorset with the 3.8pm to Axminster, Devon on 24 August 1963. Due to its severe curves, for many years three Adams 0415 class 4-4-2Ts were the only suitable locomotives to work the branch. The curves were realigned in 1960 enabling the Ivatt tanks to be used until the branch closed on 29 November 1965. The lamp standard has been adapted to hold a light at higher level. *(Author)*

Ivatt Class 2 2-6-2T No. 41320 is seen near Newton Poppleford working the 10.45am Sidmouth to Waterloo earlier on 24 August 1963. The SR used discs during the day rather than lamps and the headcode depicted the route, not the class of train. This engine, being one of the last members of the class to be built, had cylinders 16½in x 24in instead of the 16in x 24in of the earlier examples of the type. *(Author)*

Near Colyford, U class 2-6-0 No. 31798 works the 12.50pm Seaton Junction to Seaton which carries through coaches from Waterloo, on 24 August 1963. No turntable was provided at Seaton, so a locomotive had to work tender-first in one direction. Crews disliked tender-first working as they were exposed to the elements, although this could be somewhat ameliorated by a storm sheet from the cab roof to the tender. Unless the coal in the tender was well-damped, dust would blow in their eyes. No. 31798 was built as No. A798 *River Wey* by the Southern Railway in June 1925 from the South Eastern & Chatham Railway 'River' class 2-6-4T design. It was rebuilt into a 2-6-0 in August 1928 because on 24 August 1927 the Cannon Street to Deal Pullman car express headed by 'River' class No. A800 *River Cray* derailed killing 13 passengers. The inquiry found that the engines of this class were unstable except on superb permanent way, so were therefore rebuilt as tender locomotives. Nevertheless, the general manager, Sir Herbert Walker, called for a higher standard of permanent way by using the high-grade Meldon ballast to a greater depth than hitherto.

No. A798 went to Eastbourne shed and was then transferred to Redhill before it was rebuilt. By 1956, it was at Guildford and ended its days at Yeovil. The batch of U class sent to Yeovil steamed poorly, so unofficially the depot removed a modification to the blast pipe and this transformed them into good engines. No. 31798 was withdrawn in 1964 and disposed of by Bird's Commercial Motors, Morriston. *(Author)*

↑ The west portal of Venn Cross Tunnel, seen from the footplate of 4300 class 2-6-0 No. 7326 on 8 August 1963. Venn Cross station was interesting inasmuch as it lay literally on the border between Devon and Somerset, the boundary passing between the signalbox and goods shed. Situated in a cutting 666ft above sea level, it was of unusual design for the West Country as the station offices were at the top of the cutting rather than by the platform. The trap point is there to deflect any movement not obeying the signal and the '40' sign warns of a 40mph speed limit. *(Author)*

↗ Southern N class 2-6-0 No. 31838 rests at Barnstaple Junction locomotive depot on 8 August 1963, while an Ivatt Class 2 2-6-2T stands below the lifting gear, with a GWR 0-6-0PT beyond. Coal and ashes lie on the ground and were often used as filling for slipped embankments. The N class Moguls were the predecessors of the U class and had 5ft 6in driving wheels instead of 6ft. *(Author)*

→ Ivatt Class 2 No. 41297 is on station pilot duty at Barnstaple Junction in June 1963 coupled to WR coaches. This LMS design 2-6-2T continued to be built by BR for use by the SR and WR and were well liked by locomotive crews as they were fast and economical. The line which curves sharply to the right led to Ilfracombe, while No. 41297 is proceeding past Barnstaple 'B' signalbox, towards Bideford. *(R. E. Toop)*

A '43XX' 2-6-0 at Wiveliscombe in June 1962 heads a Barnstaple to Taunton train, with the brick-built goods shed beyond. The signalman is probably waiting outside his box to exchange single-line tablets. A trickle from the injector can be seen below the footplate. The 4300 class was a tender version of the 3150 class 2-6-2T and were very versatile engines capable of dealing with both freight and passenger trains, and even express passenger workings on occasions. They had a nautical roll at speed. *(R. E. Toop)*

Waiting at Minehead with a Paddington train on 17 August 1963 is 5101 class 2-6-2T No. 4143, correctly carrying the express headcode. The platforms are capable of taking 16-coach trains and the canopy is about 350ft in length. The platform edges have been recently whitened and the turntable road can be seen on the left. The station is conveniently sited on the sea front and is as busy as ever today being the terminus of the popular West Somerset Railway. *(R. E. Toop)*

Collett 1400 class 0-4-2T No. 1421 at Hemyock having arrived with the 1.42pm from Tiverton Junction on 8 August 1963. Behind the train, left, is a water tank. Speed over the branch was insufficient for the axle-driven dynamos to keep the batteries charged and so branch coaches continued to be gas lit. Following closure of the BR gasworks at Exeter in 1962, it was decided that rather than convert the existing low-loading gauge coaches to electric lighting, two ex-LNER brake second coaches, which were found to be suitable, were used for the winter of 1962–63. The battery problem was solved by linking them to a charger at Tiverton Junction. In the foreground is a trap point to catch any milk tankers running away from the creamery, situated behind the photographer. *(Author)*

A 4575 class 2-6-2T, No. 5563, is seen at Durston on 2 June 1962. The first engine of this class appeared in 1927 and was an improved version of the 4500 class which had been introduced in 1911, with increased water capacity, and therefore weight. The sleeper crossing at the platform ends looks tempting for passengers, but a notice warns that it is not for public use. The water crane has a 'devil' to prevent freezing in frosty weather and nearby, to the left of this is the concrete ramp of an end-loading platform for wheeled traffic. A train of vans is in the background. *(R. E. Toop)*

'Small Prairie' No. 5563 is seen again at Durston on 2 June 1962. The brake van is branded 'Castle Cary R.U. Not in Common Use'. The signalbox is unusual in that it is set at right angles across the very wide platform. *(R. E. Toop)*

◥ An up Cheddar Valley train headed by a 2-6-2T is at Congresbury, the junction with the Wrington Vale branch. On the platform is a travelling safe to carry the station's daily takings to the district cashier at Bristol Temple Meads. Stations en route would place money in a leather cash bag sealed with string and sealing wax bearing the station stamp. Alternatively, a small brass padlock was used. The bag was posted through a non-returnable flap. On the wall is a BR map and two new posters advertising holiday resorts. The building on the right is of typical Bristol & Exeter Railway design with elaborate barge boards and at the far end of the platform, left, is a 15mph restriction board. *(R. E. Toop)*

◀ BR Standard Class 3 2-6-2T No. 82037 at Shepton Mallet High Street on 1 September 1962, heading for Wells. The town's importance is expressed by the covered footbridge. At the foot of the platform ramp are stands for speed restriction signs. An up train is leaving the other platform for Witham, while in the siding on the right are a number of steel-carrying wagons. The right-hand home signal protects a crossover from the down siding to the up main which allowed up trains to be signalled away from either platform. This was useful as it permitted a goods train to be shunted out of the way to allow an up train to pass. *(R. E. Toop)*

↑ Bristol Barrow Road (82E) Ivatt Class 2 2-6-2T No. 41208 shunts at Wrington on 22 October 1962. This infrequently photographed branch line originally ran from Congresbury to Blagdon. It lost its passenger service on 14 September 1931 and goods trains were cut back to Wrington from 1 November 1950, with the entire branch closing on 10 June 1963. It was laid as a light railway with ungated level crossings and flat-bottomed rails spiked directly to the sleepers. *(Author)*

⬆ Ivatt Class 2 2-6-2T No. 41240, which went to Bath Green Park new and then transferred to Bristol Bath Road, is seen at Cheddar on 28 May 1960. The station had a train shed due to its importance – many trippers used it to visit the gorge and caves, and until 1925 it possessed a refreshment room. The building, left, is adorned with typical Bristol & Exeter barge boards. *(R. E. Toop)*

⬈ No. 41240 leaves Cheddar heading a train towards Wells with the Mendip hills rising to the left. During the season, there was heavy strawberry traffic from Cheddar and the adjoining stations, three special trains being despatched daily in the height of the season, in addition to all other trains carrying as much of this traffic as possible. A mouth-watering scent lingered after a train had passed. *(R. E. Toop)*

South Coast, London & East Anglia

The opening of the Swanage branch in 1885 improved transport between Wareham and Swanage. In the pre-railway era the horse-drawn omnibus took 1½ hours for the journey, but the first train took only 22 minutes. For much of its life the carriage of china clay provided regular traffic for the branch, while latterly a terminal at Furzebrook dealt with oil from the Wytch Farm oilfield. During the Second World War two mobile guns were stationed on the line, with two K10 class 4-4-0s manned by military personnel to move them. In the mid-20th century, local trains were push-pull worked, but through trains, such as from London, were worked by tender engines, with Bulleid Light Pacifics appearing from the early 1950s. Too long for the Swanage turntable, they had to work one way tender-first.

On 5 September 1966, 'Hampshire' DEMUs took over, but BR withdrew passenger services on 3 January 1972 and most of the track south east of Furzebrook was lifted. Subsequently, the Swanage branch has been reopened as a heritage railway which flourishes, particularly as a park-and-ride station was opened at Norden, considerably easing the difficulty of finding somewhere to leave a car at Swanage.

Bournemouth enjoyed fast steam trains from Waterloo until 10 July 1967 when third-rail electrification took over and there was no more steam on the SR. On the same date, Southampton also lost its steam service. At Southampton the port and railway grew together and on 18 September 1843 Far Eastern and West Indian mails were transferred from Falmouth, while liners had started using the port the previous year. In 1845, cross-Channel packets began running to the Channel Islands and France. The London & South Western Railway purchased the docks in 1892, these being the only ones in the British Isles capable of being entered by any vessel at any state of the tide.

Until the early 1930s, Southampton Central station was beside the bank of the River Test, but in 1934 the New Docks were opened on recovered land and placed the station ½ mile from the water. Boat trains were run to and from Waterloo for the arrival and departure of the regular Channel packets and also for such vessels as *Queen Mary* and the *Queen Elizabeth*. In 1953, an ocean passenger terminal opened, handling 650,000 in its first year. In addition to passengers Southampton handled cargo such as coal, cement, fruit, meat and wool. Due to the coming of the railway Southampton's population grew from 34,108 in 1851 to 204,707 in 1961.

Nearby, Eastleigh was built as a railway town. Towards the end of the 19th century, the LSWR's works at Nine Elms was inadequate, so in 1891 the carriage and wagon shops were moved to Eastleigh. The locomotive works followed allowing the land vacated at Nine Elms to be used for new low-level goods lines. In 1898 200 acres of farmland between the Waterloo to Southampton main line and the branch to Portsmouth was purchased. In addition to the works, a new locomotive depot was built to replace Northam shed. This new shed opened at Eastleigh in January 1903, but construction of the works was slower. By the end of 1909 350 men were carrying out loco repairs, but the main move from Nine Elms took place during January 1910, this being completed by the last day of the month. The works, planned by the locomotive superintendent Dugald Drummond, turned out its first new engine on 12 September 1910.

Recycling is nothing new and the structure of the boiler shop at Nine Elms, which only dated from 1892/93, was re-erected at Eastleigh, as were many of the machine tools. Following the Armistice in 1918, government surplus machinery was acquired cheaply and aided production.

The move to Eastleigh brought housing problems. When the carriage and wagon department moved there the local private housing was so poor that a public inquiry had to be held. Then, the transfer of footplate crews from Northam to Eastleigh was delayed, although the housing shortage was then eased by the LSWR building 54 cottages. The locomotive works move affected 1,500 men and their families and a dearth of housing caused many men to lodge in nearby towns and villages and commute to Eastleigh. On Saturdays at midday, the LSWR ran a special to Waterloo taking men to visit their families for the weekend with a corresponding train returning to Eastleigh on Sunday evening. The situation was improved somewhat when the LSWR built a further 100 cottages.

Apart from housing, the LSWR considered other aspects of its workforce's welfare. A dining hall held 600 men, while clerical staff enjoyed their own dining room. The LSWR

Institute provided a large meeting room with educational and recreational facilities for its 1,000 members. To cope with the influx, the LSWR donated £500 towards the enlargement of the parish church and gave £50 to each of the nonconformist chapels. No new steam locomotives were built at Eastleigh after 1950, although between 1955 and 1961 Bulleid 'Pacifics' were rebuilt there.

At one time, the Isle of Wight was blessed with 45¼ route miles of railway and at Grouping the Southern Railway took over the 18 locomotives, 90 coaches, 26 other coaching vehicles and 584 goods wagons. Due to the difficulty and expense of transfer to and from the mainland, these were period-pieces. The SR upgraded the system and brought in bogie non-corridor coaches hauled by O2 class 0-4-4Ts. Line closures began in 1952 and all freight services ended on 16 May 1966. The remaining line, from Ryde Pier to Shanklin was electrified and re-opened on 20 March 1967 using ex-London Transport tube stock.

Railways on the Isle of Wight mainly radiated from Newport and although route mileage was limited it was owned by as many as seven companies at one time. A serious problem was caused by heavy traffic in summer, but light traffic in winter, requiring equipment to lie idle in the latter season. Most passengers to the island used Cowes, disliking the 2,700ft walk along Ryde Pier. This was partly ameliorated by a parallel pier being built for a horse tram service from the Pier Head to the Esplanade, but the trouble of transfer from ship to tramway and then tramway to railway was still a disincentive to use this route. The answer was to construct a third pier alongside the pedestrian pier to carry a railway to the Pier Head. This was done jointly by the LSWR and the London, Brighton & South Coast Railway which both had interests in Portsmouth, from where the ferries ran. The construction of this line then made Portsmouth the main point of departure for the island and by 1929, two million passengers travelled annually on the SR-owned ferry. Although the Ryde Pier to Shanklin line is now electrified, it is good that some of the character of the island's railways are preserved in the Isle of Wight Steam Railway which runs from Smallbrook Junction to Wootton.

On 1 August 1882, the LBSCR line was extended from East Grinstead through Horsted Keynes and Sheffield Park to Culver Junction just north of Lewes, on the Tunbridge Wells line. The electrification of the Horsted Keynes to Haywards Heath line caused most passengers from Horsted Keynes to Brighton to travel via Haywards Heath, so traffic on the Sheffield Park line became light. Passenger services were advertised to be withdrawn on 13 June 1955, but due to a railwaymen's strike, last trains ran on 28 May 1955. Legally minded residents discovered a clause in the authorising Act which guaranteed four trains daily, so BR was forced to reopen the line to passengers from 7 August 1956. Trains were deliberately put on at inconvenient times and only stopped at the stations named in the agreement. BR sought Parliamentary permission to close the line and this occurred on 17 March 1958. It was not the end of the 'Bluebell Line' as a preservation society purchased the section between Horsted Keynes and Sheffield Park, re-opening this stretch in 1960 as the Bluebell Railway. At the time of writing it is being extending to meet the national rail system at East Grinstead.

The Rother Valley Light Railway opened for passengers from Robertsbridge (on the Tunbridge Wells to Hastings line) to Tenterden on 15 April 1903, extending to Headcorn on the Redhill to Ashford line 15 May 1905, by which time it had become the Kent & East Sussex Light Railway. It was unprofitable in the 1920s and went into receivership in 1932 and was operated by W. H. Austen, who as successor to Lt Col Stephens, managed a group of light railways. It became part of BR in 1948 and remained important for goods traffic and hop-pickers' trains. Regular passenger services were withdrawn on 4 January 1954 and on the same date Tenterden to Headcorn closed completely. Hoppers' trains continued to run from Robertsbridge to Bodiam until 1959 and the KESR closed completely on 12 June 1961. Preservationists took over the line and gradually reopened the sections.

By the time railways were built, London had developed to such an extent that land in the City was built on and would have been prohibitively expensive to purchase. This meant that most railways had to construct their terminus on cheaper land and so formed a ring of stations around Central London, these stations eventually linked by the underground's Circle Line.

Originally, the GWR had intended sharing the London

& Birmingham Railway's Euston station, but then decided to make an independent station at what was the suburban village of Paddington. The first station was in timber, but in 1851-53 a splendid new station and hotel was built a little to the east. The three roofing spans were augmented by a fourth in 1916.

Between the First and Second World Wars trading estates grew, light industry placed in pleasant, or fairly pleasant surroundings rather than amidst the smoke and grime of a city. One of these was at Slough which was served by its railway, the Slough Estates Company that provided locomotives for shunting the sidings.

The Midland & Great Northern Joint Railway was the largest of the English joint railways and was formed in 1893 when the MR and Great Northern Railway purchased various lines mostly in Norfolk, Cambridge and Lincolnshire. The line to Sheringham carried holidaymakers in through trains from the North and Midlands, and the GNR even provided through services from London to Cromer, although its route was 174 miles compared with the Great Eastern's 139. With Grouping in 1923 the MGNJR was run by the LMS and LNER, but in 1936 the LNER took over day-to-day administration. In the 1950s, road transport took much holiday traffic and BR could ill-afford the wage demands of 1958. Economies had to be made, so most of the MGNJR was closed on 2 March 1959. Sheringham station stayed open, but closed on 2 January 1967 when a new station was built east of the level crossing, although it later reopened with the North Norfolk Railway, now a flourishing tourist line.

⬆ M7 class 0-4-4T No. 30108 propels the 5.20pm Poole to Swanage south of Worgret Junction on 4 May 1963. The apparatus on the left side of the smokebox is a pump to provide compressed air when the driver is controlling the train from the leading coach on push-pull workings. The white disc is the route code; the lamp has a red slide for use when it is at the rear of the train. No. 30108 was withdrawn in May 1964. *(Author)*

⬆ Seen resting at Bournemouth West on 1 June 1963 is M7 class 0-4-4T No. 30127. Above the bogie can be seen the battery box providing power for the automatic warning system (AWS). No. 30127 was one of the very few pre-Grouping locomotives fitted with this equipment. When new, as No. 127, it had three coal rails on its bunker, but two more were added subsequently to increase the coal-carrying capacity by about 5cwt. A backing of metal sheeting prevented small coal falling between the bars. The cab was satisfactory in all weathers: it provided good protection in inclement weather and as the firebox back was lagged, the cab was reasonably cool in hot weather. No. 30127 was withdrawn in November 1963. *(Author)*

↗ Bournemouth on 1 July 1967, the last day of steam on the Southern Region. The depot had been re-modelled in the mid-1930s and closed with the end of steam. Rebuilt 'West Country' class Pacific No. 34004 *Yeovil* is in fair condition, but has had its nameplate and crest removed. Although generally good engines, as originally built they were not without faults, one being the chain-driven valve gear. The chain was enclosed in an oil bath and the oil leaked on to driving wheels and rails. When rebuilt this valve gear was replaced by the more usual Walschaert's type and the air-smoothed casing was removed. (Some believe their appearance was improved without it.) *(Rev. Alan Newman)*

→ Rebuilt 'West Country' class Pacific No. 34021 *Dartmoor* with no nameplate or numberplate brackets, at Bournemouth on 1 July 1967. The crane is for coaling. Part of a tool van can be seen to the left of electro-diesel No. E6039. A 'West Country' was similar to a 'Merchant Navy' Pacific, but was almost 2in shorter, had smaller cylinders and was lighter, giving better route availability. *(Rev. Alan Newman)*

Rebuilt 'Merchant Navy' class Pacific No. 35030 *Elder-Dempster Lines* in spotless condition, but without nameplates, at Bournemouth motive power depot on the last day of Southern steam, 1 July 1967. Locomotives of this class were speedy and well-liked by crews, and although as was the case with this wheel arrangement, when starting they tended to sit back on the pony truck leaving the driving wheels with less adhesion than on a 4-6-0. *(Rev. Alan Newman)*

BR Standard Class 4 2-6-0 No. 76054 at Southampton Central heading the 4.44pm Portsmouth to Cardiff on 4 July 1961. The crew seem to be looking out for the guard's 'Right away' as all passengers are on the train. No. 76054 worked the train to Salisbury where a WR engine, No. 7925 *Westol Hall*, took over. *(Author)*

Rebuilt 'Merchant Navy' class Pacific No. 35005 *Canadian Pacific* working the 13.00 Waterloo to Plymouth, on 4 August 1964, near Buckhorn Weston Tunnel. Unlike the 'West Country/Battle of Britain' Bulleid Light Pacifics, all 30 'Merchant Navys' were rebuilt. No. 35005 is now preserved on the Mid-Hants Railway. *(Author)*

⬆ 'West Country' class Pacific No. 34106 *Lydford* with the 08.20 Ilfracombe to Waterloo on 4 August 1964. This rather grubby engine in unrebuilt form has emerged from Buckhorn Weston Tunnel and is at the summit of a mile of 1-in-100 rising gradient, but despite this, steam still trickles from the safety valve. *(Author)*

↗ BR Standard Class 5 4-6-0 No. 73080 *Merlin* approaches Southampton Central with an up train on 20 April 1966. When some members of the 'King Arthur' class were withdrawn, nameplates were transferred to 20 BR Standard Class 5 locomotives working on the Southern Region. The signal gantry is simply splendid. Electrification is just round the corner and this evocative scene was soon to change. Dockyard cranes point skywards on the horizon. *(Rev. Alan Newman)*

➡ A very grubby BR Standard Class 4 2-6-4T, No. 80134, comes off an up train at Southampton Central on 13 February 1967. Although the South Eastern & Chatham Railway 'River' class tank engines of this wheel arrangement were unstable, this characteristic did not affect BR, LMS or LNER examples. *(Rev. Alan Newman)*

BR Standard Class 5 4-6-0 No. 73029 at Eastleigh shed on 13 February 1967. Apart from a sprinkling of ash in front of the smokebox, for the period the locomotive is fairly clean. The smokebox numberplate is homemade and a shed plate is lacking. *(Rev. Alan Newman)*

American-built 0-6-0T No. DS 233 at Eastleigh shed on 13 February 1967. Before allocation to the Engineer's Department, this locomotive was No. 30061, 'DS' standing for 'Departmental Southern'. Of US Army Transportation Corps design, it was purchased by the SR in 1946 for use in Southampton Docks and fitted with a modified cab and bunker. It was a member of the USA class. Three domes on the boiler look odd to British eyes, the front and rear ones being sandboxes. Some coal seems to be stored on the cab roof! It is believed that the rust patch in the centre of the side tank was caused by paint being continually chipped off when the engine was being watered. *(Rev. Alan Newman)*

'West Country' class Pacific No. 34005 *Barnstaple* at Eastleigh shed 13 February 1967. Its nameplate and smokebox numberplate have been removed and the smokebox door newly repainted. The cut-out handholds in the smoke deflectors are clearly visible. The engine is fitted with electric lights and behind the centre one on the bufferbeam can be seen the battery box for the AWS. The locomotive and tender tyres are rusty, indicating that the engine has not been moved for a while. *(Rev. Alan Newman)*

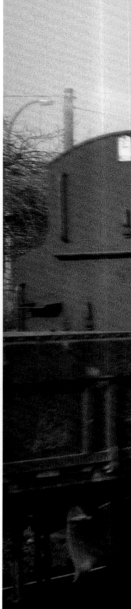

BR Standard Class 4 2-6-0 No. 76057 at Eastleigh shed on the same day, minus number and shed plates on the smokebox door. It has a straight-sided S2A pattern tender, not offering good visibility when running in reverse, but holding more coal for longer runs. This locomotive has rusty tyres so has not been used recently. *(Rev. Alan Newman)*

BR Standard Class 5 4-6-0 No. 73119 *Elaine* is another of those to have received its name from a withdrawn 'King Arthur'. It is leaving Eastleigh with a train for Waterloo on 13 February 1967. Towards the rear of the train there is a signal gantry with all semaphore arms removed. The electrified third rail can be seen in the foreground which has been laid for electric traction to replace steam power later in the year. *(Rev. Alan Newman)*

BR Standard Class 4 2-6-4T No. 80151 hauls a freight at Eastleigh, also on 13 February 1967. Steam is issuing from the injector. No. 80151 has been preserved and is operational on the Bluebell Railway. *(Rev. Alan Newman)*

⬅ On 9 August 1962, O2 class 0-4-4T No. W30 *Shorwell* working the 2.24pm Newport to Ryde, waits at Havenstreet to cross a train. Unlike many mainland locomotives of the period, Isle of Wight engines were always kept clean, although *Shorwell*'s boiler could be shinier. All the O2s on the Isle of Wight were named – an unusual feature for a tank engine at this time. The Westinghouse brake pump is prominent on the side of the smokebox, which fed the reservoir on the tank top. From 1932, the island 0-4-4Ts were fitted with extended coal bunkers. *(Author)*

⬆ The modern-looking Ryde St John's locomotive depot on 9 August 1962 photographed from a passing train. The original building, on the other side of the line, was brick and became incorporated into the Isle of Wight Railway's works. The second shed was a corrugated iron building and the third shed, depicted here, was opened by the SR in 1930. No. W31 *Chale* is the nearest engine, with the cab of either Nos W17 *Seaview* or W27 *Merstone* peeking out on its right. A pile of ash has been shovelled from smokeboxes. Isle of Wight locomotives carried their numbers painted on the bufferbeam in the traditional manner as well as on a cast plate on the back of the bunker. *(Author)*

No W30 *Shorwell* runs round its coaches at Cowes 9 August 1962 showing its red-painted rear numberplate. The fireman has just observed and informed his driver that the 'dummy' signal was off. All engines working on the island were of the tank variety as distances run were short. They were kept in a condition where they were a credit to their cleaners. *(Author)*

⬆ Ex-North London Railway 75 class 0-6-0T No. 116 built in 1881, became LNWR No. 2650, subsequently LMS No. 7505, then 27505, and finally BR No. 58850. It was withdrawn from Rowsley in 1960 after having worked the mountainous Cromford & High Peak line, but is seen here on 31 May 1967 on the Bluebell Railway, appropriately with an LNWR observation car which was restored, but awaiting its final livery. No. 2650 was delivered to the Bluebell Railway under its own steam. No coupling link can be seen at the bunker end. The Bluebell Railway was opened in 1960, together with the Middleton Railway, the first standard gauge line to be preserved. *(Author)*

London, Brighton & South Coast Railway 0-6-0T A1X class 'Terrier' No. 55 *Stepney* at Sheffield Park on the Bluebell Railway, 31 May 1967. Originally used on London suburban services, it is said that some passengers were under the delusion that their local names such as *Stepney* were in fact the train's destination! Built at Brighton in December 1875 it has a long and exceptionally interesting history. Initially No. 55, it was renumbered 655; became SR No. B655 and withdrawn from traffic in 1925 and placed in store. Reinstated in 1927, it eventually became SR No. 2655 and was ultimately withdrawn from Eastleigh shed in May 1960 as BR No. 32655.

Some 'Terriers' could be found on other lines. The London & South Western Railway purchased two for use on the Axminster and Lyme Regis branch, but they proved insufficiently powerful to handle the heavy summer traffic and sharp curves caused them to suffer extensive tyre wear. The Weston, Clevedon & Portishead Light Railway also bought a couple and when the line closed in 1940 they were taken over by the GWR. The Edge Hill Light Railway also had two 'Terriers'. Nine are preserved in Britain and one in Canada. *(Author)*

'Battle of Britain' class Pacific No. 34086 219 *Squadron* in original form, heads the 13.00 Exeter Central to Brighton train east of Buckhorn Weston Tunnel on 4 August 1964. The lower part of the smokebox door is scorched. Originally, the 'Battle of Britain' class was intended for use on the South Eastern section of the SR and the identical 'West Country' class in the eponymous area. *(Author)*

An early preserved industrial locomotive, 0-6-0ST *Charwelton*, seen on the Kent & East Sussex Railway, on 20 December 1964 having been acquired from Sproxton Quarries, Leicestershire at the beginning of the year. It was built by Manning Wardle in 1917, builder's No. 1955. *(Author's collection)*

At Paddington c1957 a 4-6-0 'King' heads the 'Cornish Riviera Limited' – the 10.30am to Penzance. The coaches are in GWR chocolate and cream livery which the Western Region reintroduced in 1957 for its principal expresses. The first regular non-stop train to Plymouth ran on 1 July 1904 via Bristol, but the new express was transferred to the more direct route via Westbury when it opened in July 1906 and being the GWR's premier train, it used the latest stock. The train's range was increased when it carried no fewer than three slip portions: Westbury for Weymouth; Taunton for Minehead and Ilfracombe and Exeter for the Torbay line. Slipping these coaches had the advantage that the train was lighter when it faced the fearsome South Devon gradients. *(J. A. Reid)*

Slough Estates Ltd 0-6-0ST No. 5, photographed on 29 May 1968. It was built by Hudswell Clarke & Co Ltd, builder's No. 1709 of 1939. A gas holder can be seen in the background. *(Rev. Alan Newman)*

Preserved Great Eastern Railway Y14 class 0-6-0 at Sheringham on the North Norfolk Railway on 7 August 1968, in GER livery. It became LNER class J15 and its BR number was 65462. The Westinghouse compressed air brake pump can be seen just in front of the cab, which is significantly narrower than the overall width of the locomotive. Notice, too, the tender is narrower than the coaches, and the elaborate cast iron canopy support on the platform. *(Author)*

Wales

Although Wales is quite a small country, extending only about 100 miles north to south and 70 miles east to west, its railway map has three sections: North, Central and South, because the most important lines in the Principality tended to go east to west. Probably due to the mountainous terrain, there was no direct main line connecting North with South Wales. The easiest way to get from north to south was through Shrewsbury in England, either by using the Central Wales line to Swansea, or the Hereford and Abergavenny line to Newport and Cardiff.

Wales provided two important ports for Ireland: the long-established Holyhead on Anglesey served by the 'Irish Mail', and Fishguard opened by the GWR to capture traffic for Southern Ireland and also, it was hoped, ocean liner traffic as it was nearer to New York than any English port. The Fishguard–Rosslare ferry opened on 30 August 1906, 20 years all but two days after the opening of the Severn Tunnel which had eased access to and from London. The GWR widely publicised its new route to Ireland, running day excursions, (literally day excursions taking about 24 hours), from many of its stations.

The mountainous regions of North Wales were very suitable for narrow gauge railways, as apart from being cheaper to build, curves could be sharper and curves were often needed in such terrain to maintain a steady gradient, or keep to a contour line. The only BR narrow gauge line in the 1950s and '60s was the Vale of Rheidol Railway running from Aberystwyth to Devil's Bridge, 670ft above sea level and almost 12 miles inland. It was built to carry lead and timber to Aberystwyth where a half-mile long branch served the harbour. The railway's promoters also had tourists in mind.

At Aberystwyth was an exchange siding with the Cambrian Railways' main line to Shrewsbury. Just over five miles from Aberystwyth, on a ruling gradient of 1 in 48 it commenced the climb to Devil's Bridge with sharp curves and several precipitous drops. The line had 2-6-2Ts and a 2-4-0T in the early days. The 2-6-2Ts were based on the Lynton and Barnstaple Railway design. Passenger traffic began on 22 December 1902. The following year, up to 20 tons of ore were despatched daily and each day of the Easter holiday 1903, over 1,000 passengers experienced travelling over the line. A halt was opened at Lovesgrove to serve an army summer camp and traffic increased to such an extent that *Palmerston*, a Festiniog Railway 0-4-0ST, was borrowed to assist working the line and at one time electric traction was seriously contemplated.

In August 1913, the Vale of Rheidol was sold to the Cambrian Railways, but the mines closed during World War One and tourist traffic declined. The GWR took over the line in 1922 when it acquired the Cambrian Railways. The following year the GWR built two 2-6-2Ts to much the same design as the originals and withdrew the 2-4-0T in 1924. The 1920s saw tourist traffic developing with open coaches generally used in summer and closed stock in winter. The daily passenger service was withdrawn on 1 January 1931 and the line only worked in summer with freight working ending on 26 September 1937. As a World War Two economy measure the line closed on 31 August 1939 until 23 July 1945. Freight was re-introduced on that date and lasted until 1 June 1964. The Vale of Rheidol locomotives were the only BR steam engines to appear in the standard blue livery with the double arrow logo. The last BR steam working over the line was a Santa Special on 18 December 1988 and the Brecon Mountain Railway company took over the railway in 1989.

The Brecon & Merthyr Railway linked Brecon with Newport. The first stretch opened was on 1 May 1863 from Brecon to Pant on the outskirts of Dowlais. It climbed over the Brecon Beacons via the Seven Mile Bank which rose 925ft in that distance, including 6½ miles at 1 in 38 – a severe test for any engine and also its brakes in the opposite direction. Passenger trains were allowed 28–30 minutes to make the 7¼-mile climb from Talybont to Torpantau and freight trains 44 minutes. Times for the descent were 15 minutes and 35 minutes respectively.

Dowlais was not the final destination as the Brecon & Merthyr had eyes on Newport. Matters were delayed by the financial crisis of 1866 when the railway's contractor, Thomas Savin became bankrupt. In addition to building the line towards Merthyr, he also worked the opened line from Brecon with his own locomotives and guaranteed a five per cent dividend. Fourteen of his locomotives eventually became the property of the Brecon & Merthyr Railway. The B&MR finally reached Newport on 1 September 1868.

The Brecon to Newport passenger service was withdrawn on 31 December 1962 and the track lifted. The formation between Pant and Torpantau was acquired by the Brecon Mountain Railway company and a 1ft 11¾in tourist line opened on 18 June 1980.

The trunk line in South Wales, the South Wales Railway, opened from Gloucester to Swansea 18 June 1850 and to Haverfordwest 2 January 1854. Between Newport and Llanelly a maze of lines, the densest network in the United Kingdom outside London, ran northwards to serve numerous colliery towns and villages, sometimes two railway companies squeezing into just one narrow valley. Fortunately, the gradient was generally in favour of loaded trains which progressed down the valleys en route to ports for onwards transport by sea, or a destination reached by rail. The opening of the Severn Tunnel on 1 September 1886 offered a more direct route to London and Southampton, avoiding the long way round via Gloucester.

A feature of many South Wales railways was their bridges and viaducts, such as Crumlin Viaduct spanning the Ebbw Valley, and at the time of its construction, the 208ft being the third highest in the world. Another impressive structure was the Barry Railway's Walnut Tree Viaduct which was 130ft high and 1,548ft in length. A curiosity was a massive steel bridge carrying the Cardiff Railway across the River Taff at Treforest which was used only once by a revenue-earning train. Two of Brunel's timber viaducts on the former Vale of Neath Railway near Aberdare were not dismantled until as late as 1947, outliving by 13 years the last of Brunel's Cornish viaducts.

The mountainous terrain in South Wales led to many tunnels: Festiniog Tunnel 2 miles 206yd being the longest, followed by Rhondda 1 mile 1,683yd, Merthyr 1 mile 735yd, and Caerphilly 1 mile 220yd. Ultra steep gradients were common. Apart from the Brecon & Merthyr's Seven Mile Bank, the Taff Bargoed Joint Line in 1913 used three locomotives and 40 minutes to raise a 20-wagon train up the seven miles of 1 in 40–47. One mineral branch of 1 in 18 was worked by adhesion and the steepest gradient faced by a passenger train was 1 in 22. At Main Incline on the Taff Vale Railway the 1 in 18 incline was rope-worked by a 50hp stationary engine. It was superseded in 1867 by a locomotive-worked 1 in 40 gradient. The Llanelly Railway's Great Mountain branch included a half-mile long balanced incline at 1 in 12 worked until c1947. At the Taff Vale Railway's Pwllyrhebog incline out of the Rhonda Valley, the half-mile long gradient of 1 in 13 was worked by three 0-6-0Ts which had a sloping firebox crown to maintain the depth of water over the firebox. Their wheels were necessarily 5ft 3in diameter to enable the axles to clear the sheaves of the winding cable. At the head of the 1 in 13, the gradient eased to 1¼ miles at 1 in 29. At one time three old tenders coupled together were kept at the incline to act as a counterbalance so that a train at the foot of the incline could ascend without having to wait until a loaded train was available at the summit. The incline closed on 1 July 1951, the three engines being withdrawn shortly after, one of which had achieved a remarkable 943,197 miles in the 67 years of short trips. Unlike most engines absorbed by the GWR, none was 'Great Westernised'.

An interesting feature following the withdrawal of steam from the Western Region, was that enthusiasts in South Wales could continue to enjoy the sight, sound and smell of steam as many of the collieries still had their own steam locomotives for internal use, sometimes ex-GWR locomotives still carrying their GWR numberplates.

➡ BR Standard Class 4 4-6-0 No. 75027, formerly used on the Somerset & Dorset line, at Llangollen with an up train from Barmouth to Ruabon on 14 August 1963. No. 75027 is now preserved on the Bluebell Railway. The station is now the headquarters of the Llangollen Railway. Notice the loading dock and siding near the typical GWR brick-built signalbox. Access to the station from the road was at footbridge level, but the booking hall and waiting room are below the bridge at platform level on the up side. The station is built on a reverse curve with platforms 734ft in length and capable of dealing with a lengthy tourist train such as were run during the eistedfodd. The further ends of the platforms, faced by the terrace of tall brick houses, were excursion platforms with ramps to dedicated exits/entrances and a further footbridge. The water tank, beyond the footbridge, is of a generous size and marks approximately the divide between the ordinary and excursion platforms. *(R. E. Toop)*

Vale of Rheidol Railway 2-6-2T No. 8 *Llywelyn* in excellent condition, except for the copper-capped chimney which needs a polish, on the BR line at Aberystwyth, 15 August 1963. Although built for the 1ft 11½in gauge, it is of typical GWR appearance and was constructed by that company. More unusual features are the centre buffer/coupler and side chains and the stone guard is in one piece rather than one for each rail as was standard gauge practice. *(Author)*

Vale of Rheidol No. 8 *Llywelyn* leaving Aberystwyth for Devil's Bridge in August 1966. The level crossing is ungated and a porter holds the traffic with a red flag. At that date it was the only passenger-carrying narrow gauge railway operated by BR. *(R. E. Toop)*

BR narrow gauge 2-6-2T No. 9 *Prince of Wales* on 15 August 1963 passes gangers. This was before the days of high-visibility clothing. From this point, beyond Capel Bangor and starting the climb to Devil's Bridge, the scenery becomes dramatic. The coaches in GWR chocolate and cream livery are of two types: saloons with windows, and saloon without glass, but with canvas, which can be seen rolled up below the eaves, or lowered in inclement weather. *(Author)*

An awe-inspiring moment where the track on a ledge high above the Rheidol Valley takes a sharp curve. You almost feel as if you are in the midst of the Rocky Mountains! *(Author)*

No 9 works hard as it hauls the coaches up the gradient of 1 in 50 round a tight curve near the summit. *(Author)*

No 9 takes a well-earned drink at Devil's Bridge before returning to Aberystwyth at the end of the outward journey on 15 August 1963. Although this locomotive is often stated to have been built by Davies & Metcalfe in 1902 for the Vale of Rheidol Railway, it was almost certainly constructed by the GWR at Swindon Works much later. *(Author)*

⬆ Collett 2251 class 0-6-0 No. 2218 pauses at Brecon on 9 June 1962 with the 2.8pm to Newport. These engines were sure-footed, with all their weight on the driving wheels, which was very necessary on this line, for it faces a climb of 6½ miles at 1 in 38 to a summit 1,314ft above sea level on one of the most exciting railway trips in the United Kingdom. Brecon station was built in a domestic style of architecture and contained the offices of the Brecon & Merthyr Railway. The platform on the left is an island, Brecon being the junction of several routes. The platform seat has cast iron legs in which 'GWR' in cursive script can be read from either side. The platform lamp is an attractive feature, but litter is in abundance on the track. *(Author)*

⬅ A 5600 class 0-6-2T, No. 5696, is seen at Dowlais on 16 May 1964, with a good heap of coal in its bunker. It is a bleak spot with a grass-covered spoil heap beyond and sheep probably grazing not far away. The engine's paintwork is typical of the period. Railways in South Wales favoured the 0-6-2T wheel arrangement which offered weight on the driving wheels – necessary for adhesion when ascending a gradient and braking when descending. Aesthetically the author has always thought that they looked like a 2-6-2T with the front wheel set removed. The '56XXs' were the largest GWR tank engines with inside cylinders. The tail lamp should have been removed from the guard's van when the engine was coupled. *(Author)*

Rhymney locomotive depot, viewed west on 15 June 1963. Opened c1864, the shed closed in March 1965, most of its allocation latterly, consisting of 0-6-2Ts. The shed is well-ventilated so the staff are unlikely to become asphyxiated. The coaling platform is on the far right and the wagons contain coal and nearby is a gantry crane. The passenger station is on the left while a goods brake van stands by the end loading dock. *(R. E. Toop)*

Rhymney shed, the view east on the same day with 5600 class 0-6-2Ts Nos. 6655 (right) and 5622. At least one 0-6-0PT is in the roofless three-road shed which measured approximately 50ft x 120ft. The office was situated at the rear of the depot and the turntable was behind the photographer. The point levers are painted white to make them more visible and less of a hazard. *(R. E. Toop)*

←Collett 5600 class No. 6643 heads the 'Rambling 56' railtour across Walnut Tree Viaduct on 31 July 1965. An ex-Merthyr fireman said that his experience of crossing the viaduct during a winter's gale required an overcoat wrapped round him because the wind was so intense. The green coach at the rear would have by its number the prefix 'S', indicating a Western Region coach maintained by the Southern Region. *(R. E. Toop)*

↑No. 6643 enters Ystrad Mynach with the 'Rambling 56' excursion. The platform on the left is composed of redundant timber sleepers and was probably slippery in wet weather. *(R. E. Toop)*

↑ Another view of the 'Rambling 56' as No. 6643 draws away from Taff Bargoed Halt and approaches Bedlinog with a good head of steam. To economise on maintenance, one road here has been lifted. *(R. E. Toop)*

➔ A final look at the 31 July 1965 '56XX' farewell railtour as No. 6643 arrives at Bargoed. A water crane is attached to the water tower, while the supply pipe to the tank is lagged with wood. Flat land is scarce – so the station offices are above the tracks. A row of fire buckets can be observed and also quite a few photographers record the scene. *(R. E. Toop)*

⬆ 'Manor' class 4-6-0 No. 7820 *Dinmore Manor* leaves Newport on 9 June 1962 with the 11.17am Cardiff to Portsmouth Harbour train. No. 7820 is now preserved and is undergoing restoration on the West Somerset Railway. Like the 'Grange' class, 'Manors' numbered 7800 to 7819 used the wheels and motion of withdrawn '43XX' class 2-6-0s but No. 7820 was built entirely new by BR in 1950. 'Manors' were lighter than 'Granges' in order to run over routes unable to support a heavier axle load and required a new design of boiler. *(Author)*

⬆ A Pontypool to Neath train is worked over Hengoed Viaduct by 5101 class 2-6-2T No. 4169 on 13 May 1961. The first member of the class was built in September 1903, but No. 4169 did not appear from the works until after Nationalisation in November 1948, while the last member of the class, No. 4179, came in December 1949. No. 4169 was withdrawn in May 1965 and cut up by R. S. Hayes Ltd. An attractive gas lamp is prominent on the left. *(R. E. Toop)*

⬆ The fireman places the stopping train headcode on 5700 class 0-6-0PT No. 4671 of 86A, Newport (Ebbw Junction) shed while at Newport, heading a train to Brecon, believed to be on 18 July 1959. Sometime in the past, the engine has worked hard and blistered the paint left of the smokebox door. On the right is a gantry with three signals while further along the train, items are about to be loaded into the guard's compartment from the trolley. *(R. E. Toop)*

↗ Hawksworth 9400 class 0-6-0PT No. 8499 acts as station pilot at Newport, probably on 18 July 1959. New in November 1952, it was withdrawn in June 1962 and unlike most earlier design pannier tank engines this class had taper boilers and the tanks did not flank the smokebox. The 'pet' pipe for cleaning the footplate and damping down coal, hangs over the cabside. *(R. E. Toop)*

➡ Ex-GWR 5700 class 0-6-0PT No. 7754 as a National Coal Board locomotive at Elliot Colliery, New Tredegar on 3 July 1967, the year the colliery closed. Built for the GWR by the North British Locomotive Company in December 1930, it was withdrawn by BR in January 1959 and sold to the NCB. It is now preserved at the Llangollen Railway. Pannier, rather than side tanks, offered easier access to oil the cylinders and motion. *(Rev. Alan Newman)*

Bristol & Bath *area*

The first railway to arrive in Bristol was the Bristol & Gloucestershire Railway, a mainly horse-worked line carrying coal from collieries nine miles north of the city. This 4ft 8in gauge line opened on 6 August 1835, three weeks before the Great Western Railway received Royal Assent. That year, a Bond & Windwood's steam locomotive used on the line exploded sending parts as far as 300yd distant, when a modification had been made in order to increase its speed to make two, instead of one trip daily. Its steam was generated in tubes, not a boiler. The Bristol & Gloucestershire Railway was extended to Standish and Gloucester as the Bristol & Gloucester Railway, a broad gauge line, although mixed gauge at its southern end to accommodate Avon & Gloucestershire stock which continued to use it. On 7 May 1845 the Midland Railway leased the standard gauge Birmingham & Gloucester Railway and the broad gauge Bristol & Gloucester Railway. The latter was duly converted to mixed gauge and the first MR standard gauge trains worked to Bristol on 29 May 1854.

The GWR line from Bristol to Bath opened 31 August 1840, but incomplete works on Box Tunnel to the east of Bath prevented it from opening the line through to Paddington until 30 June 1841. A westwards extension of the GWR was called for, this being the Bristol & Exeter Railway which opened through to Exeter on 1 May 1844 and was eventually absorbed by the GWR, on 1 August 1876.

Weston-super-Mare was one of the first seaside resorts to be served by a railway. In 1844, 23,000 visitors arrived by rail, a 300 per cent increase over the coaching era five years previously. At first, Weston-super-Mare was served by a terminal branch from the main line, but traffic grew to such an extent that in 1884 a loop line was opened. Additionally, the four-platform Locking Road Excursion station was used mainly in summer. On a typical Bank Holiday Monday the GWR and LMS brought in over 30,000 passengers in 30 special trains. Interestingly, LMS engines worked such trains between Bristol and Weston-super-Mare.

Yatton, set approximately midway between Bristol and Weston-super-Mare, was the junction of branches to Clevedon, the Cheddar Valley and Wrington, but the Beeching cuts of the 1960s reduced it to the status of an ordinary through station.

Avonmouth, six miles down stream from Bristol, was initially served by the Bristol Port Railway & Pier Company,

opened 6 March 1865 and was quite separate from other railways in Bristol. A jointly owned GWR and MR link line, the Clifton Extension Railway, opened to freight on 24 February 1877 concurrently with a new dock at Avonmouth. Due to defective track and signalling, the Board of Trade refused to pass the BPRP and CER junction for passenger working, so passenger trains from the CER could not reach Avonmouth until 1 September 1885. As ships grew too large to navigate the Avon to Bristol, Avonmouth grew in importance. Banana traffic was a principal commodity, sometimes 700 special box vans were required weekly for this traffic. Other principal commodities were petroleum, timber and animal feedstuffs. The port was vital during both world wars. The Port of Bristol Authority had its own fleet of locomotives, initially steam, but latterly diesel.

Bristol was, and is, an important rail centre, with lines radiating to Swindon, Gloucester, South Wales, Avonmouth, Portishead, Exeter and Frome; all but the last two named lines are still open. In addition, until the mid-Sixties, lines served both sides of the Floating Harbour dealing particularly with coal, timber, flour, grain and cattle. The GWR had two locomotive sheds in the city: Bath Road for passenger locomotives and St Philip's Marsh for goods, while the LMS had a shed at Barrow Road. Although most of the locomotives seen at Bristol were owned by the GWR or LMS, occasional 'foreigners' were seen such as a Great Central Railway 4-4-2 in 1903 on a through Manchester to Plymouth special, while in the 1930s SR 4-4-0s and 2-6-0s worked regularly to the city. From 1959, LNER B1 class 4-6-0s and 2-6-0s often worked to Bristol, and sometimes a V2 class 2-6-2 appeared on a freight train.

Keynsham on the main line towards Bath, apart from having water troughs, had Fry's chocolate factory, inwards traffic comprising cocoa beans, sugar and coal, while outwards came chocolate products. The factory sidings were shunted principally by a 4-wheel vertical boiler Sentinel locomotive.

Originally, the 11¼ miles of line between Bristol and Bath had eight tunnels, three of which have since been opened out. The author considers the best to be the two Twerton Tunnels with extremely attractive Tudor-Gothic arches with flanking towers like a castle portico. Four of the tunnels are Grade II listed.

Bath station, like Bristol Temple Meads, has trains on the

first floor, necessary in both cases due to the need to cross the River Avon in the vicinity. In fact, Bath station was placed between two river bridges only 700ft apart and originally cramped into that space was an engine shed, passenger station and goods depot, the latter set at right angles to the main line with access being by a wagon turntable.

The LMS facilities at Bath were extensive as they were at the intersection of lines from Mangotsfield and the Somerset & Dorset Joint Railway. As it was a terminal station, through passenger trains required a fresh engine on what had been the rear, and most goods trains were shunted, consequently Bath motive power depot had a stud of about 42 engines in the 1940s and '50s. At one time a siding led to the Avon for interchange with waterway traffic. Apart from dealing with general goods, the line served Stothert & Pitt's factory which specialised in the manufacture of cranes, while the gas works used 3,200 tons of coal weekly. Stothert & Pitt's used tractors for internal shunting, while the gas works had two steam locomotives.

⬆ Ivatt Class 2 2-6-2T No. 41245 at Yatton working the 2.45pm Bristol Temple Meads to Witham. 'SC' on the lower part of the smokebox door indicates that it has a self-cleaning smokebox. This was one of the earliest designs of the equipment and was introduced shortly before the LMS became part of BR. Internal plates and a wire mesh grid were arranged to eject through the chimney, all smokebox ash or char when the engine was working. This class of engine also had a rocking grate. Six rocking sections, divided into two groups of three fore and aft, could be rocked independently. The operating gear allowed the grate to be gently shaken when out on the road, or fully rocked for fire-dropping over a pit. Here, the fireman can be seen swinging the leather bag into the water tank. (*Author*)

↖ Weston-super-Mare, with double-chimney 'Castle' class No. 7029 *Clun Castle* left, and No. 7006 *Lydford Castle* right on 20 July 1963. It says much for the 1923 design that *Lydford Castle* emerged from Swindon Works in June 1946 and *Clun Castle* in BR days, May 1950. The latter was sent new to Newton Abbot. It was modified in the late 1950s with a high-superheat boiler and improved draughting with double chimney. She was chosen for a special fast run between Plymouth and Bristol in 1964, and secured the fastest point-to-point timings on the difficult gradients over the South Devon line. A speed of 96mph was achieved over the flatter part of the route – a record for steam which remains unbeaten. *Clun Castle* was withdrawn from Gloucester shed on 3 December 1965 having ended its days as Gloucester station pilot. It is now preserved at Tyseley. *(Author)*

← Port of Bristol Authority, 0-6-0ST No. S11 *Bristol* hauls a passenger train out of Avonmouth Docks on to BR rails. *Bristol* was built in that city in 1943 by Messrs Peckett (2036), a firm which specialised in industrial tank engines. By the number of photographers leaning out of the window, it is likely to be an enthusiasts' special. A 'mushroom' water tank can be seen above the first coach, with cranes and grain silos beyond. *(Author's collection)*

↑ In 1957, several engines were taken out of museum storage and placed in working order. These included ex-Caledonian Railway 4-2-2 No. 123 built in 1886, and GWR 4-4-0 No. 3717 (later No. 3440) *City of Truro* of 1903. They toured the country on display and are seen here at Bristol Temple Meads. *(Author's collection)*

A pleasing feature of the 1960s was the annual open day at Bristol Bath Road shed. Enthusiasts normally starved of the sight of steam in the district, could experience it here. Among the engines displayed on 21 October 1967 are ex-LMS Pacific No. 46201 *Princess Elizabeth*, left, and ex-BR (WR) No. 7029 *Clun Castle*. *(Author)*

In pre-health & safety days, enthusiasts could climb on 6100 class 2-6-2T No. 6141 in unlined livery, while on the left is a power car of the 'Bristol Pullman' set. The latter had a power car at front and rear being a precursor of today's HST. *(R. J. Cannon)*

No 46201 *Princess Elizabeth* returned for the next open day, on 19 October 1968. This view shows a close-up of the motion and cylinder. A lubricator is in front of the splasher. *(Author)*

⬆ The Bristol open day gave visitors an opportunity to have a close up look at a snow plough. Temple Meads station is on the right. *(R. J. Cannon)*

➡ The ex-LMS Barrow Road shed at Bristol on 26 September 1964. Following the closure of Bristol St Philip's Marsh shed in June 1963, ex-GWR engines were transferred to Barrow Road. Left is Class 4F 0-6-0 No. 44102 and 4-6-0 No. 4919 *Donnington Hall*, while another Class 4F 0-6-0 is shunting a parcels van, right. It looks as though the crews are changing over because one of the men has his 'traps' ie lunch, rule book, notices etc. *(R. E. Toop)*

⬆ 'King' class 4-6-0 No. 6011 *King James I* ex-works and on a running-in turn, heads a Temple Meads to Swindon stopping train over Keynsham troughs on 15 June 1957. Water sprays from the pick-up on the tender. The tank supplying the troughs is on the left. *(R. E. Toop)*

↗ A Cardiff to Portsmouth train at Newton Meadows west of Bath c1956. The GWR 4-6-0 is unidentified but the stock comes from the Southern Region. *(J. A. Reid)*

➡ Churchward 2800 class 2-8-0 No. 2811 heads a lengthy up mixed freight near Twerton Tunnel signalbox c1957. The engine is in its original condition with inside steam pipes. New in November 1905, its first shed was Bristol and it was withdrawn from Westbury in October 1959. The down track is bullhead rail, but the up has been relaid with flat-bottomed rail. The site of the up refuge siding, lifted on 12 November 1950, can be seen. When this line was constructed, a Roman villa was discovered at the far end of the cutting, and was the first important archaeological discovery made in railway building. *(J. A. Reid)*

A very welcome sight on 19 October 1963, when this line was almost entirely dieselised, was ex-LNER Pacific No. 4472 *Flying Scotsman* emerging from Twerton Tunnel with a train of Pullman coaches. *Flying Scotsman* was then owned by Alan Pegler, hence the red nameplate. *(Author)*

A down express hauled by a 'Castle' class locomotive, passes Twerton Tunnel signalbox c1956. The box closed on 20 November 1960 as part of the Bristol area multiple aspect signalling (MAS). The farmer with his tractor and roller are about to enter the ploughed field to break up the large clods of earth. *(J. A. Reid)*

An up express heads into Twerton Tunnel c1956. Evidence of the previous night's hard frost can be seen on the roofs of the coaches and the permanent way. The smoke hangs low over the train and field. Although cold, sunny weather can lead to good photographs, it can be hard to handle a camera with gloves on, and is uncomfortable to take them off. *(J. A. Reid)*

Having spent the day shunting at Bath West goods yard, 5700 class 0-6-0PT No. 9623 emerges from Twerton Tunnel into the evening sunshine with traffic for Bristol on 30 July 1963. No. 9623 was withdrawn from Bristol Barrow Road, the ex-LMS shed, in July 1965. *(Author)*

↖ Ex-US Army Transportation Corps 0-6-0T USA class No. 30073 at Bath West goods depot, en route for scrapping, on 24 May 1967. Its paintwork is in remarkably good condition for an engine going to scrap. The motion has been dismantled as was customary when an engine was hauled, to decrease the chance of a bearing running hot. The steep hill to the left of the engine is Beechen Cliff. *(Rev. Alan Newman)*

← 'West Country' class Pacific No. 34018, formerly *Axminster*, at Bath West goods depot 19 February 1968, en route for scrapping at J. Cashmore, Newport. A cab panel has been plied off. *(Author)*

↑ A dramatic scene as a down express leaves Bath Spa station c1956. Although GWR engines were not prone to slipping, a start from Bath with a heavy train could cause an engine to lose its footing due to the friction of a fairly tight curve. Above, and on the left of the viaduct, is the electricity generating station. *(J. A. Reid)*

← A 'Castle' heads an up express towards Bathampton c1956. Up and down loops enable a passenger train to overtake a freight. *(J. A. Reid)*

↑ Class 8F 2-8-0 No. 48444 heads an up freight at Twerton Turnpike west of Bath on 29 June 1964. It had only been allocated to Bath two days previously and although it looks like any other member of the class, it was actually built by the GWR at Swindon Works in June 1944 for the LMS. It was immediately loaned to the building company and did not reach the LMS until April 1947. When on the GWR it bore a number on the front bufferbeam in Great Western style, a smokebox numberplate being added by the LMS. It was withdrawn on 14 February 1966. *(Author)*

◧ Ex-Somerset & Dorset Joint Railway Class 7F 2-8-0 No. 53810 heads an up freight into the evening sunshine past Kelston Park, 16 July 1963. This engine was withdrawn on 18 November 1963. *(Author)*

⬆ Work-worn ex-S&DJR Class 7F 2-8-0 No. 53809 propels a brake van at Newton Meadows west of Bath on 19 October 1963. A cattle creep on the left allows a farmer access from a field on one side of the line across to the other. No. 53809 is now preserved at the Midland Railway–Butterley. *(Author)*

⬆ BR Standard Class 3 2-6-2T No. 82035 working the 3.40pm Bournemouth West to Bristol Temple Meads, passes the closed Weston station, Bath on 13 July 1963. The coaching set came from the SR. As was the custom with closed stations, the platform coping stones were removed. Although closed to passengers on 21 September 1953, the coal siding remained open until 29 November 1965. (Author)

➡ Class 4F No. 44264 of 82E, Bristol Barrow Road shed, is cleaned and ready to haul the enthusiasts' 'Wessex Downsman' from Bath Green Park to Bristol on 2 May 1965. Painting the reversing rod red is a pleasant touch, but colouring the buffers white, rather than burnishing them, seems a lazy option. No. 44264 was reallocated to 82E during the four weeks ending 8 September 1962 and in the week ending 12 June 1965 was transferred to 85B Gloucester Horton Road, the ex-GWR shed. An attractive MR signal is on the left. (Author)

With the transfer of Bath Green Park, from the London Midland Region to the Western Region, the ex-LMS Class 3F 0-6-0Ts which shunted at Bath were replaced by ex-GWR pannier tank engines. Here, 5700 class No. 3681 with a wooden smokebox door numberplate and looking uncared for, stands outside the motive power depot on 4 April 1965. No. 3681 was allocated to Bath in the week ending 10 October 1964 and was withdrawn on 7 March 1966. The cab and number of BR Standard Class 3 2-6-2T No. 82041 can be seen to the right. *(Author)*

Class 8F 2-8-0 No. 48525 at Bath Green Park locomotive depot c1965. This LMS engine was built by the LNER at Doncaster during World War Two and was initially used by the latter. It is seen here climbing the steep gradient from the ex-S&DJR locomotive shed. Beyond the locomotive is a water softening plant, the local water needing treatment to avoid scaling the boiler. No. 48525 was sent to Bath on 16 August 1964 on loan, which became permanent from 7 December 1964 and was withdrawn on 1 October 1965. *(R. J. Cannon)*

The smokebox and cylinder of Class 8F 2-8-0 No. 48309 at Bath Green Park motive power depot on 4 April 1965. This engine was built at Crewe during World War Two. The coach in the background belongs to a breakdown train, while beyond is the rear wall of the newly built coaling depot whose roof offers more than adequate ventilation. *(Author)*

▲ Ex-S&DJR 2-8-0 No. 53807 awaits its next duty, at Bath Green Park motive power depot on 7 June 1964. This class of engine, designed by the Midland Railway locomotive engineer Sir Henry Fowler, was ideal for working the long, steep gradients of the Somerset & Dorset, but was never replicated for use on the MR. Behind is Class 4F 0-6-0 No. 44558 built for the S&D by Sir W. G. Armstrong, Whitworth & Co. The locomotive shed was built of timber so perhaps it is surprising that it never ignited. *(Author)*

▨ A GWR intruder at Bath Green Park: 4-6-0 No. 7023 *Penrice Castle* approaches Bath Junction with an enthusiasts' special on 7 June 1964. In the 1960s, quite a number of unusual workings were arranged for enthusiasts' trains. The tracks behind the photographer are those of the S&D. *(Author)*

▨ BR Standard Class 3 2-6-2T No. 82004 and BR Standard Class 5 4-6-0 No. 73001 at Bath Green Park shed the same day. No. 82004, minus its smokebox numberplate, has 'Midford Castle' inscribed on its side tank by a humorist rubbing off the dirt. The real Midford Castle is a mock castle near the first station on the S&D out of Bath. *(Author)*

◤BR Standard Class 4 2-6-0 No. 76014 arrives at Bath with the 11.40 Bournemouth West to Bristol Temple Meads on the last day of 1964. 'Hymek' No. D7048 stands in a central siding and will probably take the train on to Temple Meads, the train having to reverse at Green Park which was a terminal station. *(Author)*

◄ BR Standard Class 4 2-6-4T No. 80059 waits at Bath Green Park with the 3.20pm to Templecombe. Its fireman is Nicky Quintain, an ex-pupil of the author. No. 80059 was an SR locomotive with lamp irons halfway up the smokebox and here it is displaying an individualistic S&D headcode. Until about the last three years of the S&D, tank engines were unknown on through Bath to Bournemouth trains, although in its early years, traffic was handled by 0-4-4Ts. In the 1960s, 2-6-4Ts shared workings with their Class 4 4-6-0 sisters. The station building, although closed to passenger traffic from 7 March 1966, has fortunately been preserved. The train shed is used for a supermarket car park, stalls and exhibitions, while the building has been developed into shops, a restaurant and a meeting room. *(Author)*

◤BR Standard Class 4 4-6-0 No. 75007 backs the 4.35pm to Templecombe into Bath Green Park on 12 October 1963. BR Standard Class 3 2-6-2T No. 82036 heads the 4.30pm to Bristol Temple Meads on the right. *(Author)*

The Somerset & Dorset Joint Railway

The Somerset & Dorset is a popular line, curiously even loved by those who never knew it. Its fascination probably grew because of the splendid scenery between Bath and Evercreech Junction; the interesting problems it posed locomotives when offering them gradients of 1 in 50, and the variety of engines used on the line.

Although the Evercreech Junction to Bath section was the most interesting, it was almost the last to be built. The S&D began with the Somerset Central Railway linking Glastonbury and Street with the wharf at Highbridge, while soon after, the Dorset Central Railway was planned to link Blandford with the LSWR at Wimborne Junction. Eventually, the DCR extended northwards to Cole and southwards to Poole, while the SCR extended southwards to Cole and westwards to Burnham-on-Sea. With ferries across the Bristol Channel and the English Channel a through route had been set up from South Wales to France. The SCR and DCR sensibly joined forces and became one company, the Somerset & Dorset Railway. Unfortunately, this through route did not lead to a boom in traffic.

In 1869, the MR opened its branch from Mangotsfield to Bath and the S&D directors saw that if they built a 26-mile extension from Evercreech, they could link with this new line and become part of a through route from the Midlands to Bournemouth and the South Coast. Skilful planning enabled the line to cross the Mendips at a height of 811ft above sea level without gradients having to exceed 1 in 50. Four tunnels with a total length of 2,576yd were required along with seven major viaducts. It speaks highly of the contractors, Messrs T. & C. Walker that they managed to build the line in the remarkable time of only two years.

This extension caused the company to overstretch itself financially. The only solution was to sell to a larger company, although in the event, two companies purchased it and ran it jointly – the LSWR and the MR. Both encouraged through traffic over the Somerset & Dorset Joint Railway between each other's systems and it prospered. Until 1930 it had its own locomotives, rolling stock and livery, but that year all engines went to the LMS, the coaching stock was divided and the SR maintained the track and signalling. In due course, the S&D was run by BR Western Region which had no interest in sending traffic over the line when it had

its own competing routes. Consequently the S&D proved uneconomic and most was closed on 7 March 1966.

Much of the fascination that the S&D has for enthusiasts is its locomotives, admirably depicted over the years by such photographers as Norman Lockett, the Rev. Alan Newman, Ivo Peters and Ronald Toop.

Summer Friday nights and Saturdays were hugely busy with a procession of trains taking holidaymakers to the South Coast and then the coaches they had travelled in used to return others home. Bath needed a large supply of engines for this, so in addition to using passenger engines, as a considerable amount of climbing was involved, freight engines were not unwelcome.

In the 1930s, locomotives used were 4-4-0s and 0-6-0s until 1938 when LMS Class 5MT 4-6-0s appeared, often piloted over the Mendips by a 4-4-0. In 1951, SR 'Light Pacifics' were tried and proved fairly successful, although no better than the 'Black Fives'. From 1951, one could see an SR engine piloted by an ex-LMS 4-4-0 or 0-6-0, and if the latter, the modern air-smoothed Pacific contrasted strongly in appearance with the goods engine.

Although the S&D 7F class 2-8-0s occasionally worked passenger trains, it was not until 1950 that they were used in emergency on summer Saturday passenger trains. They proved very useful as unassisted they could handle ten coaches over the Mendips, whereas a 'Black Five', or Pacific was limited to eight. As well as saving a locomotive, using a 7F also saved a crew. From 1952, 7Fs were allowed to work regularly on passenger trains.

These 7Fs, all 11 of the class being shedded at Bath, were also responsible for much of the interest in the S&D. Although they were Derby-designed Midland Railway 2-8-0s, they remained peculiar to the S&D, no examples ever being built for the MR's own use. They first appeared in 1914 and were so successful at their main task of taking goods trains over the Mendips, that they continued to do so for over 40 years, the first example not being withdrawn until 1959 and the last four went in 1964. This was most surprising as they were non-standard locomotives, although latterly all were fitted with the same boiler as used on LMS Compounds and the MR rebuilds. Apart from the 7F's excellent climbing ability, their braking was superb. They were fitted with Ferodo brake blocks which were relatively long-lasting and very effective on the long, steep gradients.

S&D enthusiasts also had the additional surprise and delight of seeing an engine with 'LMS' emblazoned on its tender, apparently well outside an area where one would expect to see it. In the latter years of the S&D, ex-GWR locomotives could be seen – pannier tanks shunting at Bath and 2251 class 0-6-0s working between Highbridge and Templecombe. To complete the vision of locomotives from all the 'Big Four' being seen on the S&D, LNER B12 class 4-6-0s worked ambulance trains over the line in the Second World War.

The S&D's Highbridge branch, which was largely ignored by enthusiasts, was not without interest. Although generally flat, Pylle bank consisted of about four miles in the vicinity of 1 in 100. The branch passed over peat bog and where this was particularly soft, floating frames were provided to give a firm base for the track. In one spot a narrow gauge peat tramway crossed the S&D on the level. One foggy morning as a peat locomotive was making a crossing, it became wedged across the main line. The crew of Class 3F 0-6-0 No. 3260 were unable to see it in time, it struck the disabled narrow gauge locomotive and plunged into the waterway beside the low embankment. Unfortunately, this embankment being on peat was insufficiently strong to support the two cranes required to lift No. 3260, so it had to be cut up where it lay.

At Bason Bridge, the S&D served a creamery and when most of the S&D closed on 7 March 1966 milk tank traffic from this creamery continued until 2 October 1972.

At Highbridge were the S&D locomotive and carriage works and, perhaps appropriately, had no road access. At Highbridge station the S&D crossed the GWR on the level en route to Burnham-on-Sea. Before this was reached came Highbridge Wharf which imported such commodities as timber, rails and coal, and despatched Caerphilly cheese made in Somerset and this was sent to South Wales. The S&D had its own fleet of vessels until 1934, but the Wharf was still used by other shipping until about 1950.

'West Country' class Pacific No. 34006 *Bude* on the turntable at Bath Green Park shed, 5 March 1966 having arrived with the up Locomotive Club of Great Britain's 'Somerset & Dorset Rail Tour'. *(Author)*

Class 1P 0-4-4T No. 58086 in a siding at Bath MPD on 18 May 1959. At one time, Bath to Bournemouth West expresses used to be worked by engines of this type. It was the last member of the class to be withdrawn and was sent to Gorton, Manchester, for cutting up. *(R. E. Toop)*

BR Standard Class 3 2-6-2T No. 82004 at the head of the incline down to the S&D shed at Bath c1963, with coal stacked to the limit. This engine was allocated to Bath from 24 October 1959 and withdrawn on 1 October 1965. *(R. J. Cannon)*

← BR Standard Class 4 2-6-0 No. 76027 heads SR coach set 887 on a Bath Green Park to Bournemouth West train, c1963. *(R. J. Cannon)*

↙ Ex-S&DJR Class 7F 2-8-0 No. 53807 at Bath MPD c1962. Messrs Stothert & Pitt's crane works can be seen, left, beyond the water softener. No. 53807 was the last member of the class to run in BR service and was withdrawn on 5 September 1964. *(R. J. Cannon)*

→ Class 4F 0-6-0 No. 44146 stands at Bath Junction ready to bank a train up the 1 in 50 to Combe Down Tunnel on 5 September 1960. The brake van on the left is an SR vehicle. *(Author)*

↘ Two former S&D locomotives, Class 7F 2-8-0 No. 53807 and 4F 0-6-0 No. 44558 pass Bath Junction with an up special on 7 June 1964. Coal wagons for Bath gas works can be seen beyond the 2-8-0. To enable the 7F to work this tour, it had been sent to Swindon Works for attention, possibly to valves and pistons. *(Author)*

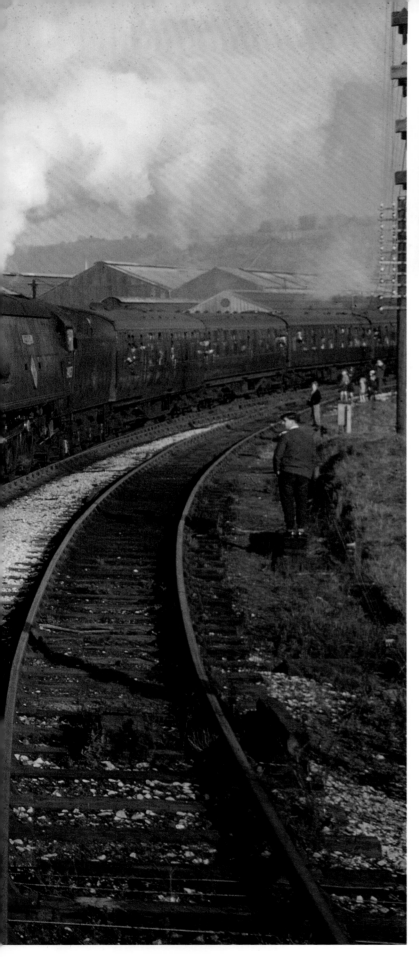

◄ Making a splendid sight, Nos 34006 *Bude* and 34057 *Biggin Hill*, pass Bath Junction on the return LCGB S&D farewell special on 5 March 1966. *(Author)*

⬆ 'Battle of Britain' class Pacific No. 34057 *Biggin Hill* (left) and 'West Country' class Pacific No. 34006 *Bude* pass Bath Junction with the up Locomotive Club of Great Britain 'Somerset & Dorset Rail Tour' on 5 March 1966. *Bude* was the engine involved in the 1948 locomotive exchanges when it was temporarily given a Stanier tender to enable it to pick up water from troughs on other regions. *(Author)*

◤ 'West Country' class Pacific No. 34102 *Lapford* starts the climb of 1 in 50 at Bath Junction with the down 'Pines Express' on 14 April 1960. This type of engine worked over the S&D from 1951. An earth slip at Midford on Monday, 5 December 1960 closed the line, so consequently, No. 34102 hauling the up 'Pines Express' was diverted via Salisbury and Bath Spa. A replacement engine was supposed to be waiting at Dr Day's signalbox, Bristol, but on arrival no engine was available. The train crew was told to go on to Gloucester where the Bulleid Pacific would be replaced. Once more, nothing was available, so *Lapford* continued to Birmingham New Street and stayed overnight at Saltley shed. The following day, it returned with the down 'Pines Express' over the same route via Bath Spa and Salisbury and when it reached Bournemouth its tender was empty. *(Author)*

◤ BR Standard Class 3 2-6-2T No. 82004 with the 18.03 Bath Green Park to Binegar on 28 June 1965. The upper part of the smokebox door is covered in rust and the engine is minus its shed plate. Apart from this train, in latter years, small tank engines on passenger trains were unusual on the northern part of the S&D. At Bath Junction the signalman hands over a bundle of large, single-line tablet pouches as many had been used due to the Bath Junction automatic tablet collector pillar, which used small pouches, being out of order. *(Author)*

◤ Climbing out of Bath to Devonshire Tunnel c1962, BR Standard Class 5 4-6-0 No. 73049 has two milk tanks 'inside' the tender, probably destined for Wincanton or Bailey Gate. They are running empty after repair, or being transferred from another milk service. Despite the gradient of 1 in 50, the engine has steam to spare. *(R. J. Cannon)*

⬆ Ex-LMS Class 2P 4-4-0 No. 40568 and a BR Standard Class 5 4-6-0 ascend the 1-in-50 Devonshire bank out of Bath with an express to Bournemouth West c1960. The bank received its name from the nearby Devonshire Tunnel, which in turn was given its name from a public house. *(R. E. Toop)*

⬈ A Bath to Templecombe train headed by ex-S&D Class 4F 0-6-0 No. 44557 leaves Midford c1954 with a rake of Southern Region coaching stock. The building on the right is a ground frame hut. Midford signalbox, seen to the left of the last coach, was rebuilt with a flat roof following reconstruction after it was partly destroyed by a runaway train on 29 July 1936. *(R. E. Toop)*

➡ Heading the 4.35pm Bath Green Park to Bournemouth West on 14 May 1960, BR Standard Class 4 4-6-0 No. 75073 is seen near Midford. A few years earlier, this train would have been hauled by a Fowler Class 2P 4-4-0. *(Author)*

One of the few good things that the Western Region did for the S&D was to introduce BR Standard Class 9F 2-10-0s for passenger work in 1960. They could handle up to 12 coaches, but could not be used for freight as Evercreech Junction turntable was not long enough to accommodate them. No. 92233 was allocated to Bath in the week ending 23 June 1962. In this picture near Midford No. 92233 heads the 7.45am Bradford to Bournemouth West on 18 August 1962. *(Author)*

At Midford, BR Standard Class 4 4-6-0 No. 75009 pilots S&D Class 7F 2-8-0 No. 53810 with the Cleethorpes, Lincoln and Nottingham, to Sidmouth and Exmouth train on 18 August 1962. The Eastern Region and Southern Region provided coaching stock in alternate weeks. This train only ran on Saturdays, the coaches remaining in Devon for a week. Up and down trains crossed at Bath Green Park. After this date, only two more trains ran on this service before the withdrawal of through passenger workings over the S&D. No. 53810 was withdrawn on 18 November 1963. *(Author)*

BR Standard Class 4 4-6-0 No. 75027 working the 4.20pm Bath Green Park to Bournemouth West on 2 June 1962 has steam to spare as it leaves Midford up a gradient of 1 in 60. The SR three-coach set No. 971 is strengthened with another bogie vehicle and a four-wheeled van as tail traffic. *(Author)*

↑ BR 4-6-0 No. 75027 again, with 'West Country' class Pacific No. 34041 *Wilton*, work the 10.30am Liverpool to Bournemouth West near Midford on 18 August 1962. No. 75027 is preserved. *(Author)*

↗ Class 4F 0-6-0 No. 44102, minus its shedplate, and 'West Country' class No. 34043 *Combe Martin*, near Midford with the down 'Pines Express' the same day. The headboard was placed on the Pacific and so is obscured in this view. No. 44102 was allocated to Templecombe on 20 December 1947, transferred to Bath Green Park in the four weeks ending 2 November 1963, and withdrawn on 1 September 1964. *(Author)*

➡ BR Standard Class 4 4-6-0 No. 75071 heads the 4.35pm Bath Green Park to Bournemouth West, passing under an occupation bridge near Midford on 23 June 1962. The coal is piled unusually high in the tender. *(Author)*

BR Class 4 4-6-0 No. 75009 between Midford and Wellow, working the 3.20pm Bath Green Park to Templecombe on 2 June 1962 with SR coach set No. 966. This design of tender was particularly suited for tender-first running. *(Author)*

Class 2P 4-4-0 No. 40697 and a BR Standard Class 5 4-6-0 pass Writhlington Colliery with an express to Bournemouth West. *(R. E. Toop)*

Lord Salisbury, a National Coal Board 0-6-0ST built by Peckett (1041) in 1906, shunts at Norton Hill Colliery c1960. A Class 3F 0-6-0T is at the other end of the train. Until 1 January 1947, *Lord Salisbury* worked at Coalpit Heath Colliery, north east of Bristol. *(R. E. Toop)*

⬆ Sister Class 2P 4-4-0 No. 40698 passes a permanent way hut as it ascends the 1 in 50 between Radstock North and Midsomer Norton South on 19 May 1956. Running almost parallel, but down near the valley floor, is the ex-GWR Bristol–Radstock–Frome line. *(R. E. Toop)*

➡ Class 4F 0-6-0 No. 44557, an ex-S&D locomotive, climbs the 1 in 50 into Midsomer Norton South station in May 1962. The 4Fs being sure-footed, proved very useful for hauling passenger trains over the Mendip Hills. In these days of stress on safety, the sleeper crossing appears perilous and today, the rural background is now covered with buildings. *(R. E. Toop)*

Class 3F 0-6-0T No. 47557 shunting at Midsomer Norton South, working under a loading gauge, which is still there today. The station, famed for its flowers, has in recent years, been re-opened and the track re-laid. No. 47557 was allocated to 22C, Bath in the week ending 21 March 1942, and withdrawn on 14 February 1964. *(R. E. Toop)*

The highly attractive Midsomer Norton South station viewed from the brake van of an up train on 5 September 1960. The train is headed by BR Standard Class 5 4-6-0 No. 75071. The signalbox was demolished but has recently been recreated as a perfect replica. *(Author)*

At Midsomer Norton South, a Class 3F 0-6-0T has removed two vans from an up express passenger train. The ex-LNER van in front of the engine is labelled 'Fruit'. *(R. E. Toop)*

↑ A down express to Bournemouth West passes Moorewood Sidings with 2P 4-4-0 No. 40634 and a BR Class 5 4-6-0 in charge. Although climbing at 1 in 60, hardly any exhaust shows. The sidings were taken out of use on 9 December 1964. On the left is a permanent way hut constructed from old sleepers, with a brick-built chimney. *(R. E. Toop)*

← Class 2P 4-4-0 No. 40700 and BR Standard Class 5 4-6-0 No. 73050, which was exhibited at Willesden in 1953, head the down 'Pines Express' near Chilcompton on 19 June 1954. The side of the cutting, right of the leading engine, appears to have given trouble. No. 73050 is now preserved on the Nene Valley railway and is named *City of Peterborough*. *(R. E. Toop)*

↗ Class 7F 2-8-0 No. 53801 works the 9.53am Bath Green Park to Bournemouth West between Binegar and Masbury c1954. Although definitely a freight engine with 4ft 8½ in diameter driving wheels, from 1950 members of this class were used on summer Saturdays when the S&D was very busy and there was a dire shortage of locomotives and crews. A 7F could haul ten coaches, whereas Bulleid Pacifics and 'Black Fives' were restricted to eight. On one occasion, a 7F made two double trips between Bath and Bournemouth in a day, 286 miles. It is interesting to observe the three green SR coaches in the middle of the seven-coach formation. *(R. E. Toop)*

➡ A down freight train climbs the 1 in 63 to Masbury summit behind BR Standard Class 5 4-6-0 No. 73047 on 5 September 1960. The signal arm has a sighting board behind it to improve visibility. *(Author)*

The up 'Pines Express' at Masbury summit, 811ft above sea level. It is hauled by Class 2P 4-4-0 No. 40568 and BR Standard Class 4 2-6-0 No. 76013. With a trailing load of 12 coaches, the engine crews have had a task climbing the gradient and it speaks highly for them that both engines are blowing off. *(R. E. Toop)*

Class 2P 4-4-0 No. 40700 approaches Masbury summit with a down train on 28 August 1954. The green ex-London & South Western Railway coach set No. 346 has a maroon coach trailing. *(R. E. Toop)*

BR No. 75071 climbs the 1 in 50 at Masbury Halt c1960 with a Templecombe to Bath Green Park train. Masbury was an isolated station and became a halt when staff was withdrawn on 26 September 1938. If travelling from Bath to Wells, it was quicker to get off the train at Masbury and travel the 3½ miles by road, rather than change at Evercreech Junction and then at Glastonbury, making a rail distance of 22¾ miles. *(R. E. Toop)*

Ex-GWR 2251 class 0-6-0 No. 3210 at Evercreech Junction backing on to the 9.55am mixed train to Highbridge on 13 April 1963. The van is plated 'Fruit'. Although following Nationalisation, the S&DJR was operated by the London Midland Region and the Southern Region, the Western Region took over on 1 February 1958 and ex-GWR engines appeared on the line. The track rises towards the goods sidings, which are level. The centre road held engines which assisted heavy passenger trains over the Mendips to Bath. *(Author)*

No. 3210 of 82G, Templecombe, on arrival at Highbridge East with the 9.55am from Evercreech Junction on 13 April 1963. Highbridge East 'C' signalbox can be seen in the distance, centre left and the locomotive shed and former S&D locomotive and carriage works beyond the rear of the train. To the left of the signalbox stands another 0-6-0 coupled to a brake van. *(Author)*

On the same very wet day, with escaping steam hanging low, 2251 class No. 3216 heads the 2.20pm Highbridge to Templecombe train at Highbridge East. The Bristol to Exeter main line passes under the bridge on the left, adjacent to the S&D Highbridge 'A' signalbox, which closed in 1914. *(Author)*

A similar view to that on the previous page, with 2251 class No. 2219 (82G, Templecombe) in lined-green passenger livery with the final BR crest, standing at the ex-S&D Highbridge East station on 16 June 1962, with a train to Templecombe. It is surprising that at such a late date the station still has five platform faces serving four roads, excluding the two platforms on the ex-GWR main line. This ex-GWR engine carries the S&D passenger train headcode. *(R. E. Toop)*

2251 class no. 3210 leaves Highbridge Wharf and is about to cross the A38 road on the level, on 16 June 1962. Highbridge East 'A' signalbox, along with 'B', closed on 16 May 1965. *(R. E. Toop)*

Ex-LMS Class 4F 0-6-0 No. 44272 at Bason Bridge creamery on 16 June 1962 with a train of milk tanks. The vehicle next to the tender is an ex-LMS six-wheeled 'Stove R', which contained a stove for cooking. *(R. E. Toop)*

← Another Collett 0-6-0, No. 2204, is seen at Highbridge with a train from Highbridge Wharf on 16 February 1962. It is about to cross the Bristol to Exeter main line on the far right. The wharf closed to goods 2 November 1964, the same date as the ex-GWR Highbridge yard ceased operating. At one time, the S&D owned a fleet of ships and the wharf was kept very busy. The van here is of SR origin and a Ford car waits at the crossing. There is a hand-operated crane in the former GWR goods yard, right, and railwaymen's allotments are in the left corner. The signalbox, Highbridge East 'B', closed on 16 May 1965. *(R. E. Toop)*

↑ The end of the line, with Class 3F 0-6-0 No. 43427 at Burnham-on-Sea on 22 August 1959. This locomotive was involved in the Charfield smash; travelling northwards with a train of empties, when it ran into the wreckage of a crash on 13 October 1928. The regular passenger service to Burnham was withdrawn on 29 October 1951, but excursion trains continued to work to the resort until 8 September 1962. Beyond the buffer stops, left, the line used to continue down the jetty to reach a ferry to Cardiff. Goods wagons were raised and lowered along this line by a wire rope. In later years, the pier line was used by the lifeboat on its cradle. The once rail-served lifeboat shed still survives, in commercial use. *(R. E. Toop)*

Central England

Only a few sample lines can be shown in this complex area, covered chiefly by the MR and GWR. One line taken over by the GWR was the Oxford, Worcester & Wolverhampton Railway, the 'Old Worse & Worse'. Intended to be a broad gauge line from a junction with the GWR at Oxford and linking with standard gauge lines in the Black Country, the 92-mile long mixed-gauge line opened in 1854, although in the event, no broad gauge trains ever ran over it. Not an outstanding financial success, it amalgamated with the Newport, Abergavenny & Hereford Railway and the Worcester & Hereford Railway to become the West Midland Railway and was amalgamated with the GWR in 1863. Didcot to Worcester was one of the GWR's principal main lines.

Kingham was an important junction on this line where the route from Cheltenham joined, as did that from Banbury and King's Sutton. The Banbury & Cheltenham Direct Railway was used by the 'Ports to Ports Express', an unofficially named train which ran from South Wales to Newcastle-upon-Tyne. It operated from May 1906 until September 1939 and North Eastern Railway and GWR coaches were used on alternate days. Although termed 'express' it took eleven hours to travel from Swansea to Newcastle. Bourton-on-the-Water and Stow-on-the-Wold stations were originally of half-timbered construction, but in the 1930s were rebuilt in an excellent Cotswold stone design, with stone tiled roof. Although through trains from Cheltenham to Paddington travelled via Gloucester and Swindon, the shortest, quickest and cheapest route from Cheltenham to London was over the Banbury & Cheltenham Direct, changing trains at Kingham.

Hereford was an important railway junction. As we have seen, it was on the line from Newport and this was carried on northwards as a joint GWR and LNWR line to Shrewsbury, giving the Great Western access to the North of England and also forming the best link between North and South Wales. A line came in from Worcester via Ledbury, another from Grange Court south of Gloucester, and Ross-on-Wye. The MR was not left out in the cold as it had a line from Brecon.

One highly scenic line was that traversing the Wye Valley from Monmouth to Chepstow. Boring the 1,190yd-long Tidenham Tunnel took almost two years, progressing at about two yards daily. The line opened on 1 November 1876. By the late 1950s the branch had become uneconomic losing about £13,000 annually. The passenger service was withdrawn 31 January 1959, goods traffic ending five years later. Monmouth Troy station was also served by trains from Hereford and Pontypool Road.

Gloucester was an important rail centre. The Birmingham & Gloucester Railway approached from the north via the Lickey Incline. The Birmingham & Gloucester was a standard gauge railway when other contemporary lines in the area were broad gauge. Thus Gloucester became notorious for the 'break of gauge' where goods and passengers had to be transferred from one railway to another. From Swindon came the broad gauge Cheltenham & Great Western Union Railway. One of the reasons for building this line was so that in summer the excess butter produced in the area could be sent to the London market instead of deteriorating in the heat and having to be sold as grease.

Care for the environment is not just a modern concept for Squire Gordon of Kemble saw it written into the CGWUR Act that the company should plant the virgin cuttings and embankments 'in an ornamental manner with good and sufficient shrubs and forest trees.' Perhaps not so public spirited was the clause that forbade a public station on his estate or within 50yd of his boundary without his consent in writing. He also insisted on a tunnel through his grounds where only a shallow cutting was really required.

To satisfy Squire Gordon's needs, Kemble station merely had platforms and no road access, which was unnecessary anyway as they were only used for changing trains to or from the Cirencester branch. In 1881, an agreement was made with Miss Gordon that a station could be built as long as it sold no intoxicating liquor. A delightful mock-Tudor building was erected, still enjoyed by today's commuters.

Gloucester, Eastgate was the Midland Railway station. It opened on 12 April 1896 and obviated the awkward reversal in or out of the MR's terminal station adjacent to that of the GWR. As the new MR station was some distance from the GWR station it was linked by a long covered footbridge.

Unlike the Birmingham & Gloucester, the Bristol & Gloucester was originally a broad gauge line. This caused problems when the MR bought both companies as it could not run through trains from Birmingham to Bristol. Incidentally, it is not generally known that the MR at one time owned broad gauge locomotives and rolling stock. The line was converted to mixed gauge and standard gauge trains started running over the line from 22 May 1854. The broad gauge rails had to remain due to running powers granted to the GWR.

The Gloucester to Bristol line had several branches, one being that from Stonehouse to Stroud and Nailsworth. Although not perhaps so obvious today, the area was a hive of industry, particularly cloth mills worked by water power. In the 19th century manufacturing diversified into engineering, timber, printing, tanning, hair pins, walking sticks, leatherboard and bacon, which made it into a very busy and lucrative branch. Passenger traffic ended suddenly on 16 June 1947 due to a post-war fuel shortage. Originally intended to be temporary, termination of the passenger service became permanent, but freight and mineral traffic continued until 1 June 1966 when the branch closed to ease the construction of the mechanised coal concentration depot at Stonehouse.

Mill owners at Dursley saw their rivals at Stroud and Nailsworth flourish through having a railway, so set up a company to build a line from the main line at Coaley. It opened to goods 25 August 1856, but like many branches, failed financially and so was taken over by the MR in 1860. Latterly, one-coach trains sufficed. Passenger traffic was withdrawn on 10 September 1962, but general freight continued until 1 November 1966 and with the closure of R. A. Lister's private siding, the line closed completely on 13 July 1970.

From Berkeley Road a short distance south of Coaley, a line led to Sharpness and across the Severn Bridge to Lydney on the South Wales line. This branch enabled the MR to gain access to the Forest of Dean coalfield. The line's principal feature was the 4,162ft-long Severn Bridge which peculiarly, was generally little-known, despite being the longest English railway bridge, and the third longest in Britain after those spanning the Tay and the Forth. The Severn Bridge opened 17 October 1879 but was somewhat eclipsed by the Severn Tunnel opened only seven years later. Unfortunately, it was struck by an oil tanker on 25 October 1960 destroying two spans. It was decided that repair could not be justified economically and it was dismantled. Passenger services continued between Sharpness and Berkeley Road until 2 November 1964. Although the line still remains open for freight from Sharpness Docks and Berkeley power station, it is little used.

⬆ Class 5700 0-6-0PT No. 3728 at Hereford on 8 June 1963. A ramp leans against the running-in board. Below the left home signal is a calling-on arm, the diamond indicating that the line is track-circuited. The former LMS goods shed is on the right, and the GWR goods shed is on the left. The notice at the end of the platform by the signals reads: 'Passengers must not cross the line except by means of the footbridge'. (R. E. Toop)

⬆ The signals at Kingham are of an unusual pattern, being designed to allow sighting below a bridge, which is behind the photographer. No. 4100, a 5101 class 2-6-2T, built in September 1935 and withdrawn in October 1965, pulls out from the station with the 11.18am Kingham to Cheltenham St James on 15 August 1962. *(Author)*

➡ 'Large Prairie' No. 4100 is seen again, at Bourton-on-the-Water later the same day, with the 5.15pm Kingham to Cheltenham St James. A Royal Mail Morris 1000 van on the right is collecting or delivering sacks of mail. The station building was of 1930s construction in Cotswold stone, with a stone-tiled roof. The line closed on 15 October 1962 and the station building is to have a new lease of life when reconstructed at Broadway on the Gloucestershire Warwickshire Railway northern extension. *(Author)*

⬉The double-chimney 4-6-0 No. 7015 *Carn Brea Castle* approaches Kingham with the 3.10pm Worcester to Paddington express on 15 August 1962. The lines on the left curve round to Cheltenham, while behind the tall water tank is the single track to Chipping Norton, King's Sutton and Banbury. Between the station signalbox and the water tank, the line led to the locomotive shed which was closed in December 1962. At one time, the bridge in the background, left, carried trains running direct from Banbury to Cheltenham, such as the 'Ports to Ports Express'. This double-tracked line was taken out of use in September 1953, but one road was retained until 1960 to allow engine turning on the triangle. To the right of the 'Castle' is a grounded coach body. *(Author)*

⬅ Ex-GWR 4300 class 2-6-0 No. 6365 is seen at Hereford 8 June 1963 as a porter trundles a luggage trolley across the barrow crossing. Below the main signal arms are smaller calling-on signals. Carriage sidings can be seen in the distance, right. Most major stations had spare carriages at this time for strengthening trains as required. *(R. E. Toop)*

⬆Also seen at Hereford on this day was 2251 class 0-6-0 No. 2286, in lined-green livery. It is proceeding northwards over the crossover. Most British engines of this wheel arrangement carried a parallel boiler, but as this class was introduced as late as 1930, taper boilers were fitted. A four-wheeled luggage trolley loaded with a bundle of tubes consigned by passenger train service, which was more expensive, but quicker if required urgently, can be seen left. *(R. E. Toop)*

The view from the cab of Collett 7400 class 0-6-0PT No. 7403 shunting at Monmouth Troy station on 14 April 1962. The station closed to passenger traffic on 5 January 1959, which is why the signal arms have been removed. It closed completely on 12 October 1964 but the building has since been moved and reassembled at Winchcombe on the Gloucestershire Warwickshire Railway. Passengers enjoyed a pleasant rural view while waiting. The tunnel was 148yd in length. *(Author)*

Ex-GWR 0-6-0PT No. 7403 shunts the goods yard at Monmouth Troy later in the day. This class had cylinders 16½ x 24in instead of 17½ x 24in as had their ubiquitous 5700 class sisters. *(Author)*

No. 7403 then worked the Wye Valley pick-up goods stopping at St Briavels for the fireman to open the gates as the signalbox had closed in February 1959, shortly after the passenger service was withdrawn on 5 January. Opened as Bigswear, it was renamed St Briavels & Llandogo on 1 May 1909, and finally was just St Briavels from 9 March 1927. *(Author)*

After the train has traversed the crossing, it stops for the guard to close the gates. Looking back along the train it can be seen that the signal post is in situ, although the arm has been removed. *(Author)*

144 *BR Steam in the 1950s and 1960s*

⬅ 'Hall' class 4-6-0 No. 5936 *Oakley Hall* at Gloucester Central on 1 June 1963 with a 2-6-2T beyond, left. Carriage cleaning sidings are in the foreground with space-saving narrow platforms for the cleaners. A Hawksworth auto coach for the Stroud Valley service is in the foreground. The coach in the lower left corner belongs to the Eastern Region and a line of cattle trucks stand on the far side of the Prairie tank. To avoid contamination, their interiors were required to be disinfected after every journey and strict regulations were in force regarding the watering and feeding of animals in transit. The long GWR goods depot stands in the background. *(R. E. Toop)*

⬆ Auto tank No. 1424 waits at Gloucester Central on 1 June 1963 with a push-pull train to Chalford. It will return, pushing the trailer coach and although a small, antique-looking engine, the design actually dated from 1932. They had a good turn of speed and between Standish and Gloucester where the GWR and LMS ran parallel, drivers of these engines would unofficially race an LMS express, sometimes achieving speeds well over 70mph, and winning. *(R. E. Toop)*

⬉ Preserved, record-breaking GWR 4-4-0 No. 3440 *City of Truro* and 4300 class 2-6-0 No. 4358 in lined-green livery, and in excellent condition, are seen at Gloucester Central on 18 May 1957. *City of Truro* was a welcome sight when it emerged from York Railway Museum that year and earned its keep by appearing on ordinary trains in between special workings. *(R. E. Toop)*

⬅ A very grubby 'Crab' 2-6-0, No. 42872 (16A, Nottingham), stands beside Gloucester (Eastgate) signalbox. No. 42872 was withdrawn from Nottingham on 28 December 1963. To the right of the tender can be seen locomotive coal wagons on the raised line to the GWR coaling stage. The ex-GWR shed Horton Road is off the picture to the right, while the ex-LMS shed at Barnwood was a quarter of a mile further on. *(R. E. Toop)*

⬆ Collett 2884 class 2-8-0 No. 3820 near Haresfield with an up mixed freight on 11 May 1961. These engines were remarkable for the fact that they were the first 2-8-0s in Britain, being introduced in 1903 by Churchward as the 2800 class. Those built by Collett from 1936 onwards received modern features such as outside steam pipes, side-window cabs, short safety valve bonnets and whistle shields. The two tracks on the right are former GWR lines to Swindon and those on the left, the ex-LMS lines to Mangotsfield and Bristol. *(Author)*

▲ A 1400 class 0-4-2T, No. 1472, takes on water at Gloucester Central on 18 April 1963, preparatory to working the 10.20am auto train to Chalford. The funnel-shaped pillar on the left is where Fireman Bridger will place the water crane's bag after use. (Author)

◄ Before departing for Chalford, Driver Butler inspects the inside motion of No. 1472, of 85C, Gloucester Horton Road. (Author)

→ The driver's view from the cab of 1400 class 0-4-2T No. 1472 at Stroud on 18 April 1963. The low boiler and tanks permit an exceptionally good lookout and a yard crane can be seen on the right. The diamond crossover with double slip, seen in the centre of the photograph, although not rare, is an unusual piece of trackwork. *(Author)*

↘ Another view from the footplate of No. 1472 while waiting in a siding at Chalford having worked the 10.20am from Gloucester, before crossing over to the down line for the return working. Beyond the signalbox, which closed on 13 June 1965, there was a shed from 1903 until 1935 for the steam railmotor which worked the service before auto-working was introduced. In the evening, the auto coaches of the last down train of the day were stabled overnight at Chalford, the 0-4-2T returning light engine to Gloucester. The following morning, a locomotive was run light back to Chalford to work the first up service. *(Author)*

↓ The auto tank has come out of the siding at Chalford and on to the down line and is ready to push the auto coach to Gloucester Central as the 11.40am working. The guard chats to Driver Butler who is standing in the auto coach's vestibule with Locomotive Inspector Allen. The lamp, which on the trip from Gloucester would have been at the rear and displayed a red light, has had the red slide removed to show a white light. *(Author)*

⬆ In ex-works condition 5205 class 2-8-0T No. 5206 is 'wrong line' at Kemble after shunting an up train on 14 August 1962. A water crane can be seen on the right, with a water tower above. Pumps at Kemble supplied a vast quantity of water which was required for Swindon Works. As there was the danger of a burst main washing away the embankment under the track to Swindon, a 'Burst Pipe' indicator was fitted in Kemble signalbox and if it gave warning, traffic was stopped and a light engine sent out to inspect the track. Latterly, a warning was sounded at Swindon. The paving stones, lower left, have a tread in the middle to give an easier passage for porters' barrows. *(Author)*

↗ A 1600 class 0-6-0PT, No. 1664, being watered at Kemble the same day after arrival with a goods train from Tetbury. This class of pannier tank was a Hawksworth design introduced in 1949, but very much in GWR style. It was intended for light branch working and shunting and weighed only 41 tons 12cwt, about 9 tons less than an engine of the 5700 class. The fireman stands on the tank top, while the driver waits, ready to turn off the water before the tanks are overfilled. The diamond on the signal post shows that the line is track-circuited and the train's presence known in the signalbox. Kemble station is well-used today by commuters who enjoy living in the Cotswolds and do not mind the 1 hour 18 minute journey to Paddington. The Cirencester and Tetbury branches closed to passenger traffic on 6 April 1964, but goods traffic lasted to Cirencester until 4 October 1965. *(Author)*

➡ BR Standard Class 9F 2-10-0 No. 92139 of 21A, Saltley, passes Coaley on 13 June 1962 with down petrol empties, probably the 10.40am Saturdays-excepted Bromford Bridge to Avonmouth working. It carries the headcode for a train with not less than a third of vacuum-fitted vehicles connected to the engine. The driver looks back to check the train while the fireman is busy firing. The signalbox is in a good state of repair, but was closed on 14 October 1968. *(Author)*

KEMBLE
CHANGE FOR CIRENCESTER
AND TETBURY

⬆ Ivatt Class 2 2-6-0 No. 46526 leaves Coaley on 13 June 1962 with the 4.40pm to Dursley. The type of tender as fitted to this locomotive was particularly suited for branch line working where the engine spent half its working life running in reverse, the design offering good visibility and shelter from the elements. Instead of having high built-up sides, the water tank is kept low and the sides of the coal bunker are set in from the edge to afford a good view through the rear spectacle plates. The shunter's pole rests across the bufferbeam. A single passenger coach was the norm on this service. *(Author)*

➡ Ex-LMS Class 4F 0-6-0 No. 44167 at Nailsworth on 13 June 1962. At one time, Nailsworth had a very busy station, and apart from coal arriving for domestic and commercial use, salt, ice and sawdust were delivered for the local bacon factory, cattle for slaughter, waste paper for a leatherboard factory, steel, roadstone and building materials. Despatched from the station were bacon products, cattle, leatherboard and live trout. A handcrane stands in the yard, right. The branch closed to passengers 16 June 1947 during the post-war fuel shortage, but goods traffic continued until 1 June 1966. *(Author)*

The 5pm Bristol Temple Meads to Derby and York, headed by 'Jubilee' class 4-6-0 No. 45614 *Leeward Islands* passes Mangotsfield on 9 June 1962; the first coach is an ER vehicle. Access to the booking office was quite hazardous at this station as a footcrossing had to be negotiated over the up and down main lines, where a tight curve restricted visibility. The garage belongs to the stationmaster. Carson's chocolate factory is rather an eyesore in the rural scene, but provided traffic for the railway, both inwards and outwards freight, while quite a few employees travelled by rail. Between the engine and the road, the remains of the Midland Railway gasworks can be glimpsed amongst the trees. Cars in the station car park include an Austin A30 and a Morris 1000. *(R. E. Toop)*

On 13 June 1962, ex-GWR 6400 class 0-6-0PT No. 6437 passes Coaley on the down line, running light engine, probably en route to work from Berkeley Road to Sharpness. The GWR had running powers over this LMS line between Gloucester and Bristol. Introduced in 1932, this Collett-designed locomotive was intended for light passenger work and was fitted for push and pull working. *(Author)*

Withdrawn locomotives being scrapped at Sharpness in 1964. Those nearest the camera are from the Western Region. *(D. Hawkins)*

↑ Ex-LMS 'Jubilee' class 4-6-0 No. 45594 *Bhopal* at Yate with the 5.45pm Gloucester to Temple Meads stopping train in July 1961. The class received its name as the first example appeared around the time of King George V's Silver Jubilee in 1935 and was, in fact, an improved version of the 'Patriot' class. Engines were named after lands in the British Empire, admirals, naval vessels and early locomotives. At Gloucester, *Bhopal* had been taken off the Newcastle to Cardiff and Bristol express earlier in the afternoon. It was withdrawn in December 1962. *(Collection Colin Roberts)*

➡ BR Standard Class 9F 2-10-0 No. 92151 powers though Mangotsfield, on 27 June 1963 with an up freight. The direct line from Gloucester to Bath ran on the other side of Carson's chocolate factory. The path beyond the white wicket gate led to North Junction, the site of the original Mangotsfield station. Behind the tender is an 'A'-type container covered with a sheet, BR anxious to keep the contents dry and thus avoid a claim for 'Damage by wet'. Over the wall in the bottom right-hand corner can be seen the top of the groundframe box at the north end of the station. The spotters in the station yard, who later formed the Mangotsfield Railway Circle, are waiting for the Up Mail, which left Temple Meads at 7.25pm. This up freight will call at Westerleigh where it will be overtaken by the Mail. *(Author)*

South Central area

This area was covered by two important lines: the GWR and the London & South Western Railway. The GWR ran from Paddington to Bristol and burrowed through the southern end of the Cotswold Hills via the 1 mile 1,452yd-long Box Tunnel on a falling gradient of 1 in 100. There was a gap between the tunnel roof and the brick lining so faggots were placed on top of the brick arches to prevent stone falls smashing them. Parallel with the main line tunnel, and immediately to its north, was another tunnel containing a standard gauge line to take stone out of the mine. In 1938, this underground quarry was converted into a vast ammunition storage depot. A punt used to be kept outside of Corsham signalbox and periodically it was placed on a permanent way trolley and wheeled down to the east end of the tunnel and used to inspect a culvert passing below the line, 176yd inside.

When the GWR was nearing completion, Daniel Gooch, its locomotive engineer, was asked to report on the best site for a locomotive repair depot. Old Swindon was a market town on a hill, skirted by the GWR and had several advantages. It was the junction with the Cheltenham line, east of Swindon the line was flat, whereas to the west were two banks of 1 in 100 and assistant engines could be conveniently shedded at Swindon, the Wilts & Berks Canal was adjacent and connected with the Somerset coalfield and so could supply fuel and also be an emergency source of water.

Stone for building the works came from Box Tunnel and the factory walls had arches, most of which were bricked up, but the design had the advantage that should a new doorway be required, stones could be knocked out without the rest of the wall collapsing. The works came into use on 2 January 1843 with more than 423 men being employed. Initially, only intended for repair, in April 1846 the first new locomotive was built there. By September 1849 the works had doubled in size to cover 14½ acres. Over the years other products were made: rails, carriages, wagons and road vehicles, while a gas plant supplied the railway housing estate as well as the works. With an eye to economy, the GWR discontinued street lighting on the three nights either side of a full moon.

By 1892, almost 10,000 men were employed producing a new engine weekly, a new coach daily and a new wagon every working hour. In 1919, the erecting shop was almost doubled in size to cover 11½ acres, the largest permanent workshop in Europe. One of the features of the works was the annual

Trip and in 1939 this had grown to such an extent that a total of 27,000 workers and their families left Swindon in 30 special trains, leaving the town almost deserted. With the increase in car ownership, numbers using the Trip decreased and they ceased in 1960. The GWR looked after its workers and 300 cottages were built for them in 1845. The railway company provided a church, school, health facilities, a hearse and the Mechanics' Institute containing a library, theatre and lecture rooms.

The GWR was not the only railway to serve Swindon because running north and south was the Midland & South Western Junction Railway, a line linking the MR at Cheltenham with the LSWR at Andover. At one time it was claimed that passengers could travel faster from Cheltenham to London via Andover than more directly by the GWR. The line was a vital link in both world wars taking strategic goods from the Midlands to the South Coast and wounded from Southampton northwards. In 1958 trains were diverted from the ex-LMS Cheltenham Lansdown station to Cheltenham St James. This stopped the line being a convenient through route and as local traffic was insufficient to justify services, passenger traffic was withdrawn on 9 September 1961 and many stations closed completely.

Westbury station was established on the Wilts, Somerset & Weymouth Railway which ran from Chippenham and Bathampton to Weymouth, and made a junction with the branch from Salisbury. Around the end of the 19th century, the GWR was criticised for being the 'Great Way Round' and it certainly needed a shorter route between Reading and Taunton than that provided via Swindon, Bath and Bristol.

A glance at the new railway map showed a fair mileage of existing line could be used plus some new construction. The Berks & Hants Extension Railway could be used to reach Patney & Chirton where a new line would run to Westbury. From there the existing railway could be used to Castle Cary and from where new construction would take trains to Langport where a widened Durston to Yeovil branch led to Athelney. More new construction would be made to Cogload Junction where it would join the Bristol to Exeter line. This plan created a new 100-mile line for the cost of building less than 33 miles.

Salisbury is an important junction on the LSWR's line London to Exeter, being the junction with the line from Southampton and the GWR's Salisbury branch. Although the London to Exeter Central line has become less important as a

through route, indeed, it was singled in places west of Salisbury, the branch from Westbury remains important and carries traffic from South Wales to Southampton and Portsmouth.

The Longmoor Military Railway began as the Woolmer Instructional Military Railway in 1908, its name changed in 1933. It offered the experience of double and single line working and to give the opportunity of long-distance working, an oval permitted trains to keep running round and round Hornby-style. One interesting feature of the LMR was that it offered free travel to passengers, including civilians, providing they held a ticket stating that they travelled at their own risk. The LMR linked with BR at two stations, Bordon and Liss. The line closed completely on 31 October 1969.

⬆ Swindon station on 2 September 1961 and 'King' class 4-6-0 No. 6013 *King Henry VIII* heads a down South Wales express with BR Standard Class 3 2-6-2T No. 82031 as station pilot on the left. The ground floor of the building on the left was at one time occupied by the infamous refreshment rooms, while the upper floor was a hotel. On 26 March 1898 it caught on fire. Why? A wooden beam ran through a chimney and lead gas pipes were run down the flues! *(R. E. Toop)*

Box stationmaster Wilf Talbot on the up platform, 1962. Wayside stations often had attractive flower gardens. However, this could become a disadvantage because when staff redundancies were made, the authority believed that if they had time to do gardening, the station was overstaffed. *(Author's collection)*

Swindon Works from a passing train on 7 August 1964 with ex-works 4-6-0 No. 7909 *Heveningham Hall*, left, and No. 6952 *Kimberley Hall*. No. 7909 was of the 'Modified Hall' design, Class 6959, by Hawksworth with the plate frame extending to the bufferbeam and new-pattern cylinders and saddle. The bogies have plate frames and an increased wheelbase. Two 350hp diesel-electric shunters are on the right. *(Author)*

A 'foreigner' at Swindon Works: ex-LMS Class 4F 0-6-0 No. 44102. This engine was shedded at Templecombe on the S&D and was sent for repair to Bristol St Philip's Marsh. It stayed there for a long time and was eventually sent to Swindon for attention. The tablet catcher holder can be seen on the tender. Below the enormous water tank behind, is the pattern store. *(R. J. Cannon)*

The scene at Newbury on 2 September 1961 as 6100 class 2-6-2T No. 6131 is being watered at the down platform. The filler cap to the right-hand side tank is open to allow the displaced air to escape, additionally to that which finds its way out through the vent. With a tank engine you want as much water as possible and to ensure this, as well as filling the tank on the water crane side up to the brim, if the other filler cap is opened, a visual check can be made that it, too, is filled. The tank on the water crane side fills before the other, and although the tanks are connected with a pipe, it takes time for the water level to balance. A three-car dmu stands at the up platform. The centre roads are used by non-stop trains and unfortunately, the design of the canopy on the up platform obscures the architecture of the building. *(R. E. Toop)*

'Modified Hall' 4-6-0 No. 7925 *Westol Hall* at Westbury on 4 July 1961 with the 4.44pm Portsmouth Harbour to Cardiff. The signal with holes in the arm is a 'wrong road' signal. *(Author)*

Rebuilt 'Battle of Britain' Pacific No. 34090 *Sir Eustace Missenden, Southern Railway* at Salisbury MPD on 9 May 1967 looking cleaner than the average engine of the period, but like many of its contemporaries, missing the smokebox numberplate and nameplates.
(Rev. Alan Newman)

BR Standard Class 4 2-6-0 No. 76028 of 71A, Eastleigh at Collingbourne Kingston Halt on 17 April 1961 with the 1.52pm Cheltenham St James to Andover. The 'SC' plate on the smokebox door denotes 'self cleaning' smokebox, as described earlier and was a device which avoided the labour and unpleasantness of shovelling out ash. The engine is not too clean and the only things that shine are the pony truck wheel flanges. The down platform is sleeper-built. *(Author)*

Rebuilt 'West Country' class Pacific No. 34025 *Whimple*, again with nameplates removed, at Salisbury locomotive depot on the same day. Much ashpan clinker and smokebox char has been removed. On the far side of the locomotive is the coaling plant. The cable leading into the cab is for an electric inspection light for firebox and tube cleaning.
(Rev. Alan Newman)

⬆ Longmoor Military Railway 'Austerity' 0-6-0ST No. 196 and SR USA class 0-6-0T No. 30064 approach Westbury on 21 October 1966 en route for the open day at Bristol Bath Road shed. No. 30064 is now preserved on the Bluebell Railway. No. 196 arrived at Longmoor in November 1964 following a general overhaul at the Ministry of Defence Central Workshop, Bicester. It was named *Errol Lonsdale* on 8 January 1968 and worked regularly until the line closed on 31 October 1969, and is now preserved on the South Devon Railway. *(Rev. Alan Newman)*

➡ Longmoor Military Railway ex-WD 2-10-0 No. 600 *Gordon* at the open day on 28 September 1968. This locomotive is in resplendent condition, and is now preserved as a static exhibit on the Severn Valley Railway. *(Rev. Alan Newman)*

◀ LMR 'Austerity' 0-6-0ST No. 195 at Longmoor Downs on an open day, 3 June 1967, with a train for Liss. It was a pleasure at this date, when BR steam stock had a generally run-down and neglected appearance, to see well-cared for vehicles and locomotives. The coaches are ex-South Eastern & Chatham Railway. The concrete water tank was a relatively rare sight on a British railway. Longmoor was set up early in the 20th century to give railway training to soldiers. *(Author)*

◤ Another view on the LMR's 1967 open day with 0-6-0STs Nos 195 right, and 196, at Longmoor Downs station. The period ex-SECR 'birdcage' brake-third coach contrasts with the modern-style signalbox which looks like a blast-proof design. The track is relatively simple, flat-bottomed type. *(Author)*

▽ A re-railing demonstration of 2-10-0 No. 601 on the Longmoor Military Railway during the 1967 open day. It was lifted vertically and then pushed horizontally by hydraulic power supplied by a portable generator. The disc pony truck wheel was a feature of the 'Austerity' design. *(Author)*

Midlands & North-West England

North West England was interesting for its splendid scenery and also the problems it posed railways working in the area. Chester, served by the Birkenhead Joint, Cheshire Lines Committee, Great Central and London & North Western railways was, and is, an important railway centre with lines radiating to almost all parts of the country.

Crewe still has its six important junctions. The Grand Junction Railway purchased large tracts of land at Crewe in 1840 and transferred its locomotive and carriage works from Edge Hill, Liverpool, Crewe being a more central position. By 1843 the works employed 160 men and the railway built 200 homes to house them. Its successor, the London & North Western Railway built more houses, churches, schools and a mechanics' institute and provided gas, water, police services and Queen's Park. In the late Victorian era, 10,000 were employed at the works and between 1843 and 1890 an average of more than one new locomotive a week emerged from the factory. In 1908 it spread over 116 acres, 36 of those being covered. In addition to the LNWR, the town was served by the North Staffordshire Railway and the GWR. Rolls-Royce cars and aero engines later gave the town a broader-based economy.

The NSR, affectionately known as 'The Knotty' due to its emblem the Staffordshire Knot, was a profitable company, often paying a dividend of five per cent. Apart from heavy industrial traffic including coal, stone and ironstone, it carried many passengers to the North Wales coast, the nearest seaside to the Midlands. It owned a greater length of canals than any other system and unlike most other railways, developed, rather than neglected its waterways.

The Cromford & High Peak Railway was incorporated on 2 May 1825. It had eight steep inclines with gradients up to 1 in 7 worked by stationary engines with parts of the line reaching 1,000ft above sea level. Opened in 1830, it was isolated until 1853 when it was linked to the Manchester, Buxton, Matlock & Midlands Junction Railway. The High Peak line was not itself authorised to carry passengers, but they were carried, including on the inclines, by a private firm. The company was vested in the LNWR 1887. It closed in 1967.

The Middleton Railway, Leeds, was one of the first railways in England. Opened on 20 September 1758 it had a gauge of 4ft 1in and unusually for contemporary railways, was double tracked. Originally horse-worked, in 1812, to counter the soaring cost of horse fodder, two rack-and-pinion locomotives, designed by John Blenkinsop and built by Matthew Murray at Leeds, were ordered and became the first railway engines to be operated commercially. To obviate the danger of the locomotive's weight breaking the cast iron plate rails, Blenkinsop used toothed rail so the engine did not need to be heavy to give sufficient adhesion.

The locomotives were life-expired by 1835 and fodder prices had reduced, so the line reverted to horse traction until 1862 when steam power was again adopted, but using normal adhesion. In 1881, the line was converted to standard gauge. By 1958 most factories no longer used the line and in 1960 volunteers restored and operated the railway and sought traffic from private sidings serving lineside factories. It was the first preservation society to operate a standard gauge line in the United Kingdom.

Carnforth, on the LNWR's Lancaster to Carlisle line, formed a junction with the Furness Railway to Barrow and the FR and Midland Joint line to Wennington where the line became purely Midland to Settle Junction. In 1968, the redundant motive power depot was purchased to form 'Steamtown', the original hope being that locomotives for the preserved Lakeside & Haverthwaite Railway would be stabled and maintained at this depot, but the scheme was foiled when the trackbed south of Haverthwaite was taken for trunk road improvements. Today, it serves as the base for main line operator West Coast Railways.

On 21 April 1847, the double-tracked Kendal & Windermere Railway opened from a junction with the Lancaster to Carlisle main line at Oxenholme. Initially worked by the LNWR, in 1850 and 1851 it was operated by E. B. Wilson & Co, Leeds. The Kendal & Windermere then worked the line itself, but trains were often late. The Kendal & Windermere was ejected from the Lancaster & Carlisle's telegraph office at Oxenholme because it was using it as an unauthorised booking office. Eventually the K&WR was leased by the Lancaster & Carlisle in 1858, which the following year, was leased to the LNWR.

The coming of the railway changed Windermere. Near the terminus was the Windermere Hotel linked to the station by a private drive. The railway bought two types of passenger to Windermere – the rich, such as Manchester and Liverpool manufacturers who built large houses in the neighbourhood for weekend and summer use, the other was the working-class day tripper who only had time to walk the mile down to the promenade at Bowness. On Whit Monday 1883, 8,000 people arrived. Gradually, the village turned into a town, the population of Windermere-Bowness more than doubling between 1851 and 1891.

By 1910, the 'Windermere Express' linked Manchester and Windermere in 2hr 2min. At first, merely a down train Friday evenings and returning on Monday mornings, it later became a daily weekday service in both directions. From 1912 the train included an exclusive club car, only available to first class season ticket holders who had to apply to a club committee for election and were then faced with an annual subscription. The club car contained a comfortable armchair for each member, writing desks and a sherry cabinet. Withdrawn at the outbreak of the Second World War, it was never restored although the express, referred to as the 'Manchester Club Train', continued to run until 1966.

Excursion traffic on the branch was still busy in the 1950s, occasionally being so heavy that empty stock had to be stabled as far distant as Milnthorpe on the main line, 16 miles from Windermere. Goods traffic was withdrawn from 28 April 1969 and in 1973 the line was singled. This caused excursion trains to terminate at Oxenholme, passengers transferring to fleets of road coaches while the trains worked empty over the 50 miles to Carlisle for turning and servicing, and then travelled a further 50 miles back.

The Settle & Carlisle Railway was built because the MR wanted its own route to the gate of Scotland. Using tunnels and many viaducts, the 72-mile long line surveyed by Charles Sharland, managed to cross the Pennines using a gradient no steeper than 1 in 100, keeping above the 1,000ft contour for over 15 miles. The Settle & Carlisle was the last of the English main lines built by the traditional navvy using mainly muscle power. As the works were often far from civilisation, shanty towns for workmen were established with shops, public houses, bakeries, hospitals and schools. Through freight began on 2 August 1875 and passenger services from 1 May 1876. Dent station, 1,145ft above sea level, was the highest on an English main line when it opened on 6 August 1877.

Garsdale water troughs installed 1907, were the highest in the world for many years and were steam-heated against the frost. Hawes Junction, renamed Garsdale in 1932, had the famous turntable which, in December 1900, saw the wind spinning an engine round uncontrollably. To prevent a repetition, a stockade of vertically placed sleepers surrounded it. Another interesting feature at Garsdale was the social centre complete with stage, set under the water tank, and each Sunday a harmonium was wheeled into the down waiting room for divine service. A couple of miles beyond Garsdale, Ais Gill at 1,169ft above sea level, was the highest summit on an English main line.

BR Standard Class 9F 2-10-0 No. 92082 at Stoke-on-Trent motive power depot on 30 April 1967. The ash plant is on the left. *(Rev. Alan Newman)*

⬆ Ivatt Class 2 2-6-0 No. 6441 built in 1950 (BR No. 46441), was a preserved locomotive stored at Carnforth in August 1968. Restored in unauthentic livery, the author considers the style of the numerals ugly. The tender cab shows well in this view. *(R. E. Toop)*

↗ Carnforth-based Class 5 4-6-0 No. 45017, with combined dome and top feed, stands on the turntable at its home depot in August 1968. It was withdrawn that month when BR steam traction was abolished, and it went to Draper's yard in Hull where it was not scrapped until May 1969. A few more 'Black Fives' lurk in the background and on the right is Class 4MT 2-6-4T No. 42073, preserved for the Lakeside & Haverthwaite Railway. This engine was allocated to 55E, Normanton in June 1967, withdrawn in October 1967, and stored there from October 1967 until March 1968 when sent to Carnforth. The vehicles in vivid red livery are part of the breakdown train. The crane itself can be seen above the cab of the 'Black Five'. *(R. E. Toop)*

➡ Fairburn Class 4MT 2-6-4T No. 42085, stands at Carnforth in August 1968, is clean, but with aged paintwork in lined livery with the first BR crest which ceased to be applied about 1956. It was allocated to Normanton from April to October 1967 when it was withdrawn and stored until transfer to Carnforth in April 1968 for operation on the Lakeside & Haverthwaite Railway with No. 42073. The chimney is covered to keep the weather out. It is next to the tender of LNER B1 class 4-6-0, No. 61306, another locomotive retained for preservation. There were several types of LMS 2-6-4Ts. The first was the Fowler 1927 two-cylinder parallel-boiler design. In 1934, Stanier introduced a taper-boiler design with three cylinders intended for the London, Tilbury & Southend section, followed in 1935, by a similar two-cylinder locomotive. Then, in 1945, Fairburn modified it to be lighter and have a shorter wheelbase. No. 42085 is the latter design, a gap between the running plate and bufferbeam being a weight-saver. The Fairburn 2-6-4T with modifications, was adopted as the Standard BR engine, numbered in the 80xxx series. The small-wheel wagons, left, are for ash. *(R. E. Toop)*

◤ Class 3F 0-6-0T No. 47482 at Crewe South on 8 June 1966 has passed through the shops at Darlington which explains the BR number being on the tank side, as was North Eastern Region practice, rather than on the cab side. The backplate rails at the top of the coal bunker offer increased coal capacity. Crewe South shed dealt with freight engines, while Crewe North was passenger, but if short of locomotives would borrow from Crewe South. The locomotive in front of the 'Jinty' is one of the rather unattractive Ivatt Class 4MT 2-6-0s. *(Rev. Alan Newman)*

◄ Crewe South on 8 June 1966 showing, left to right: Class 5 4-6-0 No. 44669, BR Standard Class 9F 2-10-0 No. 92113, and BR Standard 'Britannia' Class 7 Pacific No. 70031 *Byron*. All are in the typical grubby condition of the period. From 1958, No. 44669 was a 12A, Kingmoor engine, withdrawn in October 1967 and scrapped by the Motherwell Machinery & Scrap Co. of Wishaw in February 1968. The writing on the bufferbeam of No. 92113 is its shed name. It was withdrawn in October 1967. *(Rev. Alan Newman)*

◤ Class 5 4-6-0 No. 45055 of Lostock Hall shed is seen at Carnforth with empty stock, in August 1968. 'Carnforth' appears to be painted on the bufferbeam. No. 45055 has an older boiler with combined dome and top feed. It was scrapped by Draper's of Hull in February 1969. The coaches are in the BR light grey and blue livery which appeared only in the latter days of steam. There is an abundance of four-wheel goods wagons in the background while a water tank almost conceals the signalbox. *(R. E. Toop)*

↑ North Staffordshire Railway L class 0-6-2T No. 2 at National Coal Board Walkden on 9 June 1966. Although built in 1923, this locomotive carried an NSR number because the railway was not taken over by the LMS until later that year. It had been restored in NSR livery for display at the City of Stoke-on-Trent Jubilee celebrations in 1960 and returned to NCB use in this livery until 1967 when withdrawn and acquired for preservation. *(Rev. Alan Newman)*

↗ Class 5 4-6-0 No. 44684 passes under the impressive signal gantry at Chester on 10 June 1966. A dmu shed can be seen on the right. In March 1964, the 'Black Five' was transferred from Crewe North to Crewe South; in June 1964 back to Crewe North, returning to Crewe South in September 1964. Withdrawn in November 1965 it was scrapped by Ward's, Beighton, Sheffield, in January 1966. The headcode indicates a through freight or ballast train. The upper lamp bracket is midway up the smokebox door, rather than in its original position at the top. This move avoided the risk of a fireman inadvertently approaching too near the wires for the overhead electrification. *(Rev. Alan Newman)*

→ Ex-Ministry of Supply 0-6-0ST No. 68006 purchased in 1946 by the LNER and classified J94. Seen here on 30 October 1963 at the foot of Sheep Pasture Incline on the Cromford & High Peak line. This was the lowest number of the class which totalled 75 examples, but many more were in industrial and military railway use. The cable-worked incline can be seen rising beyond the overbridge. One of the hopper wagons is sheeted. *(Author)*

◤ Sentinel geared locomotive LNER No. 54 – this was its number in departmental service. Previously LNER Y1 class No. 59 it was renumbered 8153 and BR No. 68153. It is seen here on the Middleton Railway on 4 August 1967. Although having the appearance of a diesel locomotive, it is steam driven and has a vertical boiler in the cab. Behind it is Bagnall 2702 of 1943, an 0-4-0ST, which is so low-slung, its buffers are above the frame. *(Author)*

◄ Ex-North Eastern Railway 0-4-0T, Worsdell H class No. 1310, built at Gateshead in 1891, seen here on the Middleton Railway, 4 August 1967. As LNER Class Y7 it was withdrawn in 1931 and sold to the coal industry, passing from the NCB into preservation in 1965. A delightful little engine, it looks as though it should have a hole to put a key in to wind it up! *(Author)*

▲ 'Austerity' J94 class 0-6-0ST Nos 68012 and 68006 head the last steam run on the Cromford & High Peak line on 30 April 1967. Some enthusiasts occupy the brake vans, while others throng the bleak lineside. *(Rev. Alan Newman)*

⬆ BR Standard 'Britannia' class Pacific No. 70038 (originally named *Robin Hood*), at Grayrigg on 16 June 1967 with an up express freight, authorised to run at a maximum speed of 35mph. *(Rev. Alan Newman)*

➡ Fairburn Class 4MT 2-6-4T No. 42299 at Windermere with the 14.00 to Kendal and Oxenholme service on 12 August 1963. Although the population of Windermere was only about 6,000, the Furness Railway station is suitably large to cater for tourists. *(R. E. Toop)*

⬆ Class 5 4-6-0 No. 44795 (12A, Kingmoor) heads a down parcels train over Dillicar troughs on 15 June 1967. The engine has plenty of steam, and a plume shows above the safety valve. No. 44795 was withdrawn in July 1967 and scrapped by McWilliams, Shettleston in December 1967. It was a joy taking colour photographs of steam engines in such surroundings. The troughs, immediately south of Tebay, was an exciting place to be. Up trains thundered down from Shap, while down trains built up speed for the four miles of 1 in 75 to Shap summit. *(Rev. Alan Newman)*

↗ BR Standard 'Britannia' class Pacific No. 70045 (originally named *Lord Rowallan*), of 12A, Carlisle Kingmoor shed, at Greenholme on 16 June 1967, with an up parcels train. *(Rev. Alan Newman)*

➡ Class 5 4-6-0 No. 44732 (8F, Wigan Springs Branch) heads an up express freight not fitted with continuous brakes, at Hardendale, on 16 June 1967. Although the engine is working hard, the safety valves are just blowing off. Withdrawn in July 1967, it was scrapped by Cashmore of Great Bridge in January 1968. *(Rev. Alan Newman)*

Carlisle Kingmoor Class 5 No. 44883, also seen on 16 June 1967, approaches Scout Green with a mixed freight, about midway up the four miles of 1 in 75 to Shap summit. It is assisted in the rear. Next to the tender is a Continental ferry wagon. *(Rev. Alan Newman)*

A few moments later, No. 44883 passes Scout Green. It is in deplorable condition and only the cabside number has been cleaned. Withdrawn in July 1967, it was scrapped by McWilliams, Shettleston in December 1967. *(Rev. Alan Newman)*

↑ BR Standard Class 9F 2-10-0 No. 92024, originally fitted with a Crosti boiler, climbs to Shap summit. The safety valves are just blowing off and the tender water filler cap has not been closed. The two white and red flashes each side of the tender, warn men of the danger from overhead electric wires which had been laid on part of the London Midland Region. The black smoke indicates that the fire is being given plenty of attention. *(Rev. Alan Newman)*

↓ The last view from the photographer's 16 June 1967 visit to the North West shows No. 92024 has passed below the bridge and BR Standard Class 4 4-6-0 No. 75039 appears, providing rear-end assistance. This class of locomotive, although broadly similar to the Class 5, had a smaller boiler and driving wheels of 5ft 8in diameter instead of 6ft 2in. This meant that it was lighter and enjoyed almost universal availability over main and secondary lines in Britain. *(Rev. Alan Newman)*

'Britannia' Class 7MT Pacific No. 70013 (formerly named *Oliver Cromwell*), passes Garsdale on 9 August 1967 with a down express freight, partly fitted with not less than a third of vacuum-braked vehicles connected to the engine. This engine is now preserved and returned to the main line in 2008 to mark the 40th anniversary of the end of regular steam on BR.

The 'Britannias' were the first of the new BR Standard types to appear, one being exhibited at the South Bank, London in the 1951 Festival of Britain. In order not to hurt the feelings of engineers in the various regions, the class was designed at Derby, built at Crewe and sections designed at Brighton, Doncaster and Swindon works. Apart from the one-off Pacific No. 71000 *Duke of Gloucester*, these were the largest express passenger steam locomotives designed and built by BR. *(Author)*

Another example of the ubiquitous 'Black Five' 4-6-0s, No. 44669 (12A, Carlisle Kingmoor) passes Ais Gill on 12 June 1967 with a Carlisle to Skipton freight. This locomotive has the final form of separate dome with the top feed well forward. It was withdrawn in October 1967 and scrapped by Motherwell Machinery & Scrap Co, Wishaw in February 1968. Netting has been erected to deter sheep from jumping the dry-stone wall. *(Rev. Alan Newman)*

Stanier Class 5 4-6-0 No. 45227 (10D, Lostock Hall) with an up ballast train south of Ais Gill on 12 June 1967, with white-painted smokebox door hinges. This boiler has a separate dome and top feed. No. 45227 only lasted for another six months, being withdrawn in January 1968 and scrapped by Draper's of Hull, in April 1968. *(Rev. Alan Newman)*

Class 8F 2-8-0 No. 48652, built by the Southern Railway at Eastleigh Works for the LMS, heads a down freight at Ais Gill on 12 June 1967. This locomotive survived for a further 12 months before scrapping by Draper's of Hull in October 1968. *(Rev. Alan Newman)*

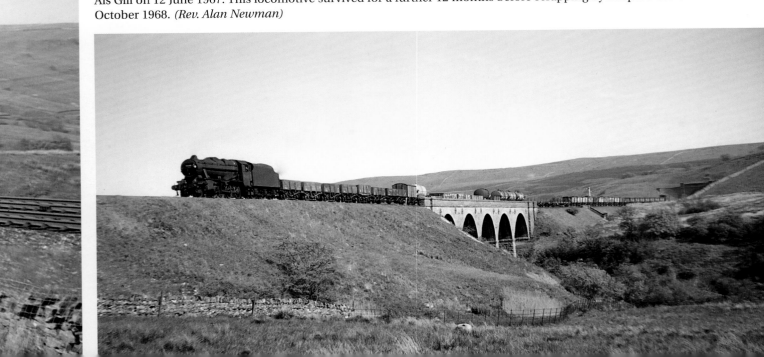

◤ Next in the procession of 'Black Fives' at Kirkby Stephen on 15 June 1967 was No. 45261 of 9B, Stockport (Edgeley), heading an up freight. Withdrawn in October 1967 it was scrapped by Cashmore's at Newport in February 1968. *(Rev. Alan Newman)*

◀ This time it was a BR Standard Class 9F 2-10-0, No. 92056, passing Kirkby Stephen during the June 1967 lineside visit. Although designed for heavy freight haulage, this class of locomotive was found to have a good turn of speed and in an emergency could work an express passenger train at speeds of up to 90mph and considered by many to be the best class of BR engine. Hopper wagons are at the rear of the train. *(Rev. Alan Newman)*

◤ An up through freight passes Kirkby Stephen on 15 June 1967 with Class 5 4-6-0 No. 44859 (5D, Stoke) in charge. Transferred to 8H, Birkenhead in August 1967, it was withdrawn in November 1967 and scrapped by Cashmore of Great Bridge in March 1968. The signal is tall to give better sighting and it bears a diamond to indicate track circuiting. The signalbox is of typical Midland Railway pattern, and has a good coal supply ready for a harsh winter. Above the first wagons of the train can be seen the top of a water tower. *(Rev. Alan Newman)*

North-East England & Scotland

North East England – the cradle of railways. Coal was relatively cheap, but heavy and bulky so needed an inexpensive method of transport from the mines to the sea. A railway fulfilled this need and at first was horse-worked, but steam locomotives proved more economic. On 27 September 1825 the Stockton & Darlington Railway opened, the inaugural train hauled by Stephenson's *Locomotion No. 1*. Coal was the principal commodity, but passengers were carried in horse-drawn coaches provided by contractors, stopping almost anywhere en route to pick up or drop off passengers. Subsequently, Darlington was placed on the East Coast route to Scotland and a branch ran to Kirkby Stephen with onwards connection to the West Coast Main Line at Tebay, or at Eden Valley Junction south of Penrith. Most of the lines in the North East belonged to the North Eastern Railway.

Sunderland and South Shields was another important area, including Ryhope on the coast just south of Sunderland. South of Ryhope stretched the Seaton branch with its gradient of 1 in 44/60 for 2½ miles. On 19 August 1889 the driver of an express descending the bank was unable to reduce its speed sufficiently to enable it to pass round the curve at its foot, the resulting derailment injuring 101 passengers. The Silksworth bank on the Sunderland to Durham line had another severe gradient causing steam locomotives to cough. Sunderland was an important rail centre, and in addition to being on the line from Hartlepool to Newcastle, lines radiated to Hendon and along both banks of the River Wear.

Newcastle Central was the most important station on the North Eastern Railway and daily handled up to nearly 1,200 trains arriving and departing. Lines radiated along the north and south banks of the Tyne in both directions, in addition to the East Coast Main Line (ECML) and branches to Sunderland, Washington and Consett.

The original ECML north of Ferryhill ran via Leamside, Penshaw, Washington and Pelaw. A more direct line was built in two sections: Gateshead to Newton Hall was opened on 1 December 1868 while the second section opened from Relly Mill Junction, Durham to a junction with the old main line two miles north of Ferryhill. This was inaugurated on 15 January 1872 thus completing the ECML that we know today. Constructing both sections required heavy engineering works including a viaduct at Chester-le-Street over quarter of a mile in length and with a maximum height of 90ft. Another viaduct over the River Wear was required at Croxdale, and one more at Langby Moor.

The Tyne Dock to Consett iron ore traffic was important, 1.25 million tons of imported ore carried over the 23 miles annually. A journey began with a mile of 1 in 40 to Bank Top, the Q7 class 0-8-0 assisted by a J72 class 0-6-0T. This was followed by about ten miles of easier gradients, but facing the chance of being delayed at level crossings, or railway crossings. From Ouston Junction the real work began with almost nine miles of rising gradient mostly in the region of 1 in 50, but with some sections as steep as 1 in 35. The final five miles undulated, but with gradients up to 1 in 54. The section between West Stanley and South Medomsley was one of the worst for severe weather.

Until November 1953, 21-ton capacity MOT steel hopper wagons with bottom discharge doors were used, a load being 22 wagons and a brake van. A Q7 class 0-8-0 could handle a maximum load of 350 tons, but with another Q7 as banker from Pelaw South the load could be 700 tons.

To render the operation more economic, unloading ships and wagons was fully mechanised, this requiring 30 new 56-ton bogie hopper wagons, each of which had two separate compartments, that were discharged by two side-opening doors. The opening was done by two compressed air engines, air supplied from Westinghouse pumps on the locomotive. The wagons were vacuum-braked. Eight wagons made up a train weighing about 700 tons. Light ore caused trouble when it got into the vacuum brake pistons, so gaiters were fitted and also leather aprons over the axle boxes to keep the dust away. Ten locomotives were fitted with Westinghouse pumps: five O1 class 2-8-0s and five Q7 class 0-8-0s, the former were train engines and the latter, bankers. From 1954 the service of ten daily trains increased to 14, working round the clock. The engine remained coupled to its train as it was turned on a triangle at Consett. When an O1 was unavailable, a Q7 was train engine, with another of the same class, but without Westinghouse pump, as banker. All the engines came from Tyne Dock shed. Train engines returned to shed after each trip, but the banking engine made three trips before returning to the shed. The use of BR Standard Class 9F 2-10-0s as train engines allowed an extra wagon to be carried.

Perhaps it is not too simplistic to say that Scotland's railways could be divided into three areas: the South relatively empty of railway lines, Central Scotland between the Clyde and Forth having a dense network, and finally the North, with railways few and far between due to both the topography and low population.

The line which perhaps most Sassenachs think of when Scotland is mentioned is that from Fort William to Mallaig. In the mid-19th century, the townsfolk of Fort William were peeved by the poor transport. A trip to Glasgow involved catching a steamer to Oban and then a train onwards. In due course the West Highland Railway was promoted to run from Craigendoran, then on beside Loch Lomond to Crianlarich and over Rannoch Moor to Fort William. The Bill was passed in 1889 and 4,000 men were engaged on its construction, many being crofters and fishermen from the Hebrides. The problems of crossing Rannoch Moor proved so costly that it was likely that the WHR would have become bankrupt but for the assistance of a rich director, J. H. Renton. To commemorate his help, his effigy was cut on a huge granite slab at Rannoch station. The 684ft long Rannoch Viaduct was built on a radius of 12 chains. In all, 350 bridges and viaducts were built on the 100 miles between Craigendoran and Fort William.

At Loch Treig a steamer was assembled from a kit of parts and transported supplies in an area with no roads. Interestingly, at Fort William the locomotive shed was built inside the outer walls of a military fort. The line opened on 7 August 1894.

The fishing port of Mallaig was isolated and welcomed a railway. By this time landowners who had hitherto objected to the building of a railway could see its advantages, so a Bill for an extension to Mallaig was passed in 1894. The Treasury, wishing to assist the Highlands, took the unusual step of guaranteeing to the railway company for 30 years, a minimum return of three per cent on £260,000.

The railway estimated that construction would take five years, but 'Concrete Bob' Robert McAlpine completed the task in just over four years. Originally a bricklayer's labourer, he made his name using concrete. The 127ft span over Borrodale Burn at the time of its construction was the world's longest concrete span. His best known structure is Glenfinnan Viaduct, 416yd in length, with a maximum height of 100ft set on a 12-chain curve. The Scottish and Irish navvies did not always agree and police block houses were wisely set up every two miles along the route. The line opened on 1 April 1901, and for some of the onlookers it was their first sight of a train. Steamers linked with Skye and Stornoway.

The railway was highly beneficial to the district. For instance, before its arrival, a trip from Mallaig to Fort William involved finding a method of travelling nine miles to Arisaig and then catching the horsedrawn coach which took 7½ hours for the 37-mile journey at a cost of £1 2s return. The new railway only charged 1s 7d more for a return ticket to Glasgow. The price of coal undercut locally produced peat. The line was a social one, partly subsidised by tax payers. The largest sum they were required to pay in any year between 1901 and 1913 being less than £4,000 and it is surprising today to realise that this expenditure aroused a political storm.

The line required special locomotives to work the long and hard gradients and traverse the curves. The 'Glen' class 4-4-0s appeared in 1913 and worked until 1959, but were assisted by K4 class 2-6-0s. In the 1950s, ex-LMS Stanier 'Black Fives' appeared on the West Highland, and also their BR Standard equivalents. Crews were critical of the LMS injector but were satisfied when it was replaced with one of LNER pattern. Alterations to the Mallaig turntable eventually allowed B1 class 4-6-0s to work to Mallaig.

Gorten Crossing on Rannoch Moor was an isolated railway community. Initially, the first train of the day offloaded 12 bucketfuls of water from the tender, but later more hygienic containers were utilised. Primary school-aged children travelled by train to school at Rannoch and those of secondary school age to Fort William. In the event of a medical emergency, a doctor travelled from Fort William on a special locomotive.

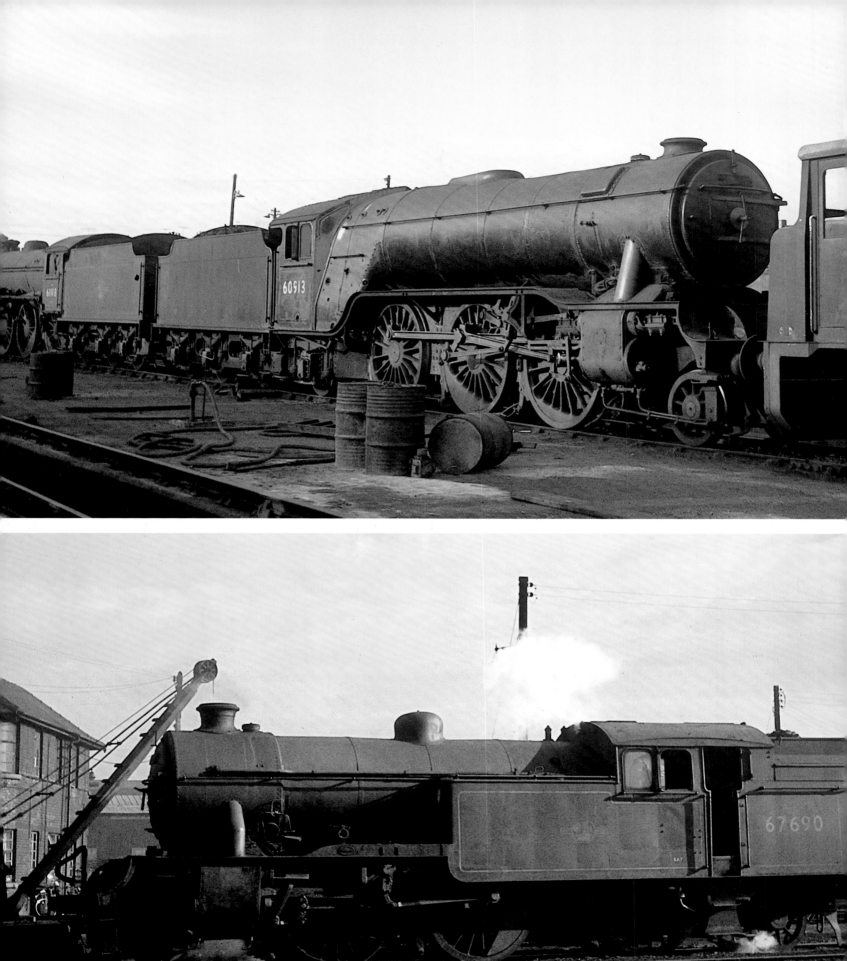

↑ Gresley V2 class 2-6-2 No. 60913 at Darlington Works on 24 October 1964. On the left is B1 class 4-6-0 No. 61118 and 0-4-0 diesel-hydraulic No. D2700 built in 1953 by the North British Locomotive Co. on the right. Both the B1 and the diesel shunter have had their coupling rods removed. *(Author's collection)*

← Also seen at Darlington on the same day was V3 class 2-6-2T No. 67690 (51A, Darlington), with a hopper-type bunker. It was withdrawn the following month. On the left is a splendid hand-worked crane. *(Author's collection)*

↑ A J27 class 0-6-0, No. 65789, is seen at Ryhope on 13 June 1967. Introduced in 1906, this North Eastern Railway class was designed by W. Worsdell and speaks highly of the design that it was still working at such a late date. The boiler is massive for an 0-6-0 and the cab gave good crew protection in inclement weather. The plate behind the coal rails on the tender is to prevent small coal escaping. *(Rev. Alan Newman)*

The number of this vacuum-fitted ex-War Department Riddles Ministry of Supply 'Austerity' 2-8-0, purchased post-war by the LNER, was not recorded, although it is possibly 90321. It was photographed at Ryhope on 13 June 1967, hauling a train of coal hoppers and obviously travelling at a fair rate. *(Rev. Alan Newman)*

Ivatt-designed Class 4 2-6-0 No. 43070 at Ryhope, also on 13 June 1967. This was one of the first batch built at Darlington in August 1950. Withdrawn in September 1967, it was stored at North Blyth until scrapped by Clayton & Davie, Dunston-on-Tyne in November 1967. The class received the nickname 'Doodlebugs', after the German World War Two flying bomb. Certainly in the Bath area, the class was disliked because of its poor steaming ability, but after No. 43094 from the Eastern Region had been on road trials from the Swindon Testing Plant, modifications were made to improve steaming.
(Rev. Alan Newman)

K1 class 2-6-0 No. 62011 passes Ryhope on the same day. Introduced in 1949, it was a Peppercorn development of the Thompson K1/1 class (itself rebuilt from a Gresley K4), with increased length. The locomotive looks in deplorable condition with the smokebox covered in rust and if a diesel had been in such a state, it would never have run. Coal has fallen into the 'four foot'.
(Rev. Alan Newman)

↑ Class J27 class 0-6-0 No. 65795 climbs Silksworth bank, County Durham on 13 June 1967, with a train of coal hoppers. The fact that the exhaust is vertical shows that the engine is working hard and the speed is slow. It is apparent that a number of glands on the locomotive are leaking, which means the fireman has to shovel more coal to replace the wasted steam. A colliery slag heap is in the background. *(Rev. Alan Newman)*

↗ Ex-WD 'Austerity' 2-8-0 No. 90417 fitted with a vacuum brake, was seen here at Ryhope the following day, 14 June 1967. The wagons immediately behind the tender are of the hopper pattern, and those further back are 16-ton mineral wagons. A shunter's pole lies across the front of the locomotive, placed through its lifting holes. Some engines of this class were built by the North British Locomotive Co. and others by the Vulcan Foundry. BR numbered the former 90000 to 90421 and the latter, 90422 to 90732 in approximate order of construction. *(Rev. Alan Newman)*

➡ Standing outside the shed at Sunderland are Q6 class 0-8-0 No. 63437 and ex-WD 2-8-0 No. 90135 on 14 June 1967. The lower part of the smokebox door of No. 63437 has become red hot at some period through drawing air through a leak, allowing oxygen to keep the smokebox cinders alight. *(Rev. Alan Newman)*

 A general view of Sunderland MPD on 14 June 1967 showing, left to right: K1 class 2-6-0 No. 62012, Q6 class 0-8-0 No. 63346, J27 class 0-6-0 No. 65855, and Q6 class 0-8-0 No. 63437. No. 65855 was built in 1908 by Beyer Peacock.
(Rev. Alan Newman)

 The tender of J27 class 0-6-0 No. 65789 being filled with water at Sunderland, this same day. A misjudgement has been made! The water crane is an interesting shape. It is not always appreciated that a steam locomotive needs to take on water more frequently than it does coal. The engine is reasonably clean seeing that it has little time left on BR. *(Rev. Alan Newman)*

 The last of the J27 class to be built was No. 65894 in 1923, seen here at Sunderland on 14 June 1967 with coal piled high in the tender. No. 65894 has been preserved and regularly featured in the credits of the television series 'Heartbeat'. *(Rev. Alan Newman)*

↑ Peppercorn A1 class Pacific No. 60149 *Amadis* has a water crane swung over the tender while it waits with an express at Newcastle Central. Oil lamps are placed on the electric lamps and the shed plate is missing. The footplate is angled to clear the driving wheels, while the splashers are very small and a plate protects the automatic warning system equipment from damage by a swinging coupling. There is a check rail on the sharp curve, left. *(Author's collection)*

← V3 class 2-6-2T No. 67691 (52A, Gateshead), the highest number in the class, at Newcastle Central on 14 August 1964, running light after shunting empty stock. It has a hopper-type bunker and the coupling and connecting rods have been painted white. On this design, one continuous splasher is above the first and second driving wheels. When withdrawn in November 1964 it was the final member of the class, and none were preserved. *(Author's collection)*

K1 class 2-6-0 No. 62023 crosses an underbridge at Pelaw on 14 June 1967 with a train of empty coal hoppers. The white and red squares on the bridge girders warn those walking along the track of limited clearance. The stanchions on the footbridge in the distance look as if at one time it was roofed.
(Rev. Alan Newman)

Another V3, No. 67638, was seen at Newcastle Central on 14 August 1964 but it has a plain, as opposed to a hopper-type bunker. Built as a V1 class in May 1935, it was converted to V3 in January 1955 and was withdrawn from Gateshead in November 1964. The V1s had a boiler pressure of 180lb per square inch and V3s 200lb psi. The water column to the right of the 2-6-2T has its leather bag wrapped around the pipe.
(Author's collection)

On 14 June 1967, K1 class 2-6-0 No. 62005 is seen at Tyne Dock MPD. Lined-out, it looks very smart with the whitened smokebox door hinges. A plate supports the front screw coupling to prevent the coupling swinging back and striking the automatic warning system equipment behind. No. 62005 has been preserved and returned to main line operating. The wagons in the background have doors opened by compressed air. *(Rev. Alan Newman)*

Departmental Locomotive No. 58, a J72 class 0-6-0T at Tyne Dock MPD, again on 14 June 1967. Built by BR as No. 69005 in November 1949, it was a development of Wilson Worsdell's NER design of 1898. Withdrawn from ordinary service in October 1964, it was renumbered in departmental stock and employed during cold weather defreezing coal wagons to facilitate tipping at the Blyth shipping staithes. This class was built over a span of 53 years between 1898 and 1951 under the auspices of the NER, LNER and BR. The tapering tall chimney, the large dome and the brass safety cover, are delightful features. Its slender appearance belied its power output. To the left of the engine is an ex-LMS brake van. *(Rev. Alan Newman)*

Resting over a pit at Tyne Dock MPD on 14 June 1967 was Q6 class 0-8-0 No. 63344, in very clean condition. The combined front sandbox and splasher flank the smokebox saddle and it has a round-topped firebox. This class of locomotive served the railway very well for 54 years. *(Rev. Alan Newman)*

← Gresley K2 class 2-6-0 No. 61787 *Loch Quoich* (65A, Glasgow Eastfield) at Fort William station on 15 August 1959. Built by Kitson & Co. in August 1921, it was named in June 1933. Withdrawn in October 1959, it was scrapped by Arnott Young, Old Kilpatrick in December 1959. All named engines of this class worked in Scotland, principally over the West Highland line to Mallaig. Most of the remainder of the ex-GNR class worked in the Lincolnshire area. The smokebox door of No. 61787 has become red hot at some period. A Morris GPO van is on the right with an AEC lorry belonging to MacBrayne's, which operated steamer services on estuaries, sea lochs and to the Isles. Some typical West Scottish rain has fallen recently. *(R. E. Toop)*

↑ A train for Glasgow leaves Mallaig on 15 August 1959, probably headed by K2 No. 61787 *Loch Quoich. (R. E. Toop)*

Index

Sheringham 55
Silksworth bank 196
Slough Estates Ltd 55
Southampton Central 41, 42
Stoke-on-Trent MPD 171
Stroud 149
Sunderland MPD 196, 199
Swindon station 159
Swindon Works 160

Taff Bargoed Halt 68
Twerton Tunnel 85, 87
Twerton Tunnel signalbox 82, 85
Twerton Turnpike 91
Tyne Dock MPD 203

Vale of Rheidol Railway 61, 63
Venn Cross Tunnel 24

Walnut Tree Viaduct 67
Westbury 163, 164
Weston station, Bath 94
Weston-super-Mare 77
Windermere 180
Wiveliscombe 27
Worgret Junction 37
Wrington 31

Yate 156
Yatton 75
Ystrad Mynach 67

Locomotives depicted

GWR/BR(W)
'City' class 4-4-0
   3440 *City of Truro* 77, 147
1400 class 0-4-2T
   1420 13
   1421 27
   1424 145
   1427 13
   1472 149
1600 class 0-6-0PT
   1664 150
2251 class 0-6-0
   2204 133
   2218 64
   2219 131
   2286 141
   3210 129, 131
   3216 129
2800 class 2-8-0
   2811 82
2884 class 2-8-0
   3820 147
4073 'Castle' class 4-6-0 17, 85, 90
   5034 *Corfe Castle* 15
   7006 *Lydford Castle* 77

7015 *Carn Brea Castle* 141
7023 *Penrice Castle* 98
7029 *Clun Castle* 77, 79
4300 class 2-6-0 27
   4358 147
   6365 141
   7326 24
4500 class 2-6-2T
   4555 13
4575 class 2-6-2T
   5525 13
   5563 28
4900 'Hall' class 4-6-0 17
   4919 *Donnington Hall* 80
   5936 *Oakley Hall* 145
   5981 *Frensham Hall* 9
   5967 *Bickmarsh Hall* 17
   5992 *Horton Hall* 11
   5994 *Roydon Hall* 17
   6952 *Kimberley Hall* 160
5101 class 2-6-2T
   4100 138
   4143 27
   4169 71
   5148 14
   5164 15
5205 class 2-8-0T
   5206 150
5600 class 0-6-2T 65
   5622 65
   5696 64
   6643 67, 68
   6655 65
5700 class 0-6-0PT
   3681 97
   3728 136
   4671 72
   7754 72
   9623 87
6000 'King' class 4-6-0 17, 55
   6011 *King James I* 82
   6013 *King Henry VIII* 159
6100 class 2-6-2T
   6131 160
   6141 79
   6146 19
6400 class 0-6-0PT
   6437 155
6800 'Grange' class 4-6-0
   6831 *Bearley Grange* 17
6959 'Modified Hall' class 4-6-0
   7909 *Heveningham Hall* 160
   7925 *Westol Hall* 163
7400 class 0-6-0PT
   7403 143
7800 'Manor' class 4-6-0
   7820 *Dinmore Manor* 70
9400 class 0-6-0PT
   8499 72

Vale of Rheidol 2-6-2T
   8 *Llewelyn* 61
   9 *Prince of Wales* 63

Southern Railway/BR(S)
A1X 'Terrier' class 0-6-0T
   55 *Stepney* (32655) 52
'Merchant Navy' class 4-6-2 (Rebuilt)
   35005 *Canadian Pacific* 41
   35030 *Elder-Dempster Lines* 41
M7 class 0-4-4T
   30108 37
   30127 38
N class 2-6-0
   31838 24
O2 0-4-4T
   W30 *Shorwell* 49, 50
   W31 *Chale* 49
U class 2-6-0
   31798 23
USA 0-6-0T
   DS233 (30061) 45
   30064 164
   30073 89
'West Country/Battle of Britain' class 4-6-2
   34006 *Bude* 104, 109
   34041 *Wilton* 116
   34043 *Combe Martin* 116
   34057 *Biggin Hill* 109
   34086 *219 Squadron* 52
   34102 *Lapford* 111
   34106 *Lydford* 42
'West Country/Battle of Britain' class 4-6-2
(Rebuilt)
   34004 *Yeovil* 38
   34005 *Barnstaple* 45
   34018 *Axminster* 89
   34021 *Dartmoor* 38
   34025 *Whimple* 163
   34090 *Sir Eustace Missenden, Southern Railway* 163

LMS/BR(LM)
Class 1P 0-4-4T
   58086 104
Class 2 Ivatt 2-6-0
   6441 (46441) 172
   46526 152
Class 2 Ivatt 2-6-2T 24
   41208 31
   41240 32
   41245 75
   41292 23
   41297 24
   41320 23
Class 2P 4-4-0
   40568 112, 127
   40634 124
   40697 119